The Defiant Muse

DUTCH AND FLEMISH FEMINIST POEMS

FROM THE MIDDLE AGES TO THE PRESENT

THE DEFIANT MUSE SERIES

The Defiant Muse: Dutch and Flemish Feminist Poems from the Middle Ages to the Present
Edited and with an introduction by Maaike Meijer; co-editors: Erica Eijsker, Ankie Peypers, and Yopie Prins

The Defiant Muse: French Feminist Poems from the Middle Ages to the Present
Edited and with an introduction by Domna C. Stanton

The Defiant Muse: German Feminist Poems from the Middle Ages to the Present
Edited and with an introduction by Susan L. Cocalis

The Defiant Muse: Hispanic Feminist Poems from the Middle Ages to the Present
Edited and with an introduction by Ángel Flores and Kate Flores

The Defiant Muse: Italian Feminist Poems from the Middle Ages to the Present
Edited by Beverly Allen, Mariel Kittel, and Keala Jan Jewell and with an introduction by Beverly Allen

The Defiant Muse

DUTCH AND FLEMISH FEMINIST POEMS
FROM THE MIDDLE AGES
TO THE PRESENT

A Bilingual Anthology

Edited and with an Introduction by Maaike Meijer
Co-editors: Erica Eijsker, Ankie Peypers, and Yopie Prins

THE FEMINIST PRESS
at the City University of New York

Published in 1998 by The Feminist Press
at the City University of New York
City College, Wingate Hall
Convent Avenue at 138th Street, New York, New York 10031

First edition

This book was published with the financial support of the Foundation for the
Production and Translation of Dutch Literature and the Prins Bernhard Fonds.

This publication was made possible, in part, by public funds from the National
Endowment for the Arts.

The Feminist Press would also like to thank Marilyn French, Celia Gilbert,
Florence Howe, Joanne Markell, Caroline Urvater, and Genevieve Vaughan
for their generosity.

Library of Congress Cataloging-in-Publication Data
The defiant muse: Dutch and Flemish feminist poetry from the Middle Ages to the
    present: a bilingual anthology / edited and with an introduction by Maaike Meijer;
    co-editors, Erica Eijsker, Ankie Peypers and Yopie Prins. — 1st ed.
        p.   cm. — (The defiant muse)
    English, Dutch, and Flemish.
    Includes bibliographical references.
        ISBN 1-55861-151-7 (alk. paper). — ISBN 1-55861-152-5 (pbk.—alk. paper)
        1. Feminism—Poetry. 2. Dutch poetry—Women authors—Translations into
English.   3. Flemish poetry—Women authors—Translations into English.
4. Dutch poetry—Women authors. 5. Flemish poetry—Women authors.   I.
Meijer, Maaike.   II. Eijsker, Erica.   III. Peypers, Ankie.   IV. Prins, Yopie.   V.
Series.
PT5475.E5D44   1998   97-34847
839.3'1100809287—dc21   CIP

Printed on acid-free paper by McNaughton & Gunn, Inc.
Manufactured in The United States of America

05 04 03 02 01 00 99 98 6 5 4 3 2 1

CONTENTS

ACKNOWLEDGMENTS

This book has been long in the making. I am grateful to my coeditors, Erica Eijsker and Ankie Peypers, who have so generously left me the anthology they had begun in the late eighties. I should like to thank the poet Elly de Waard, who was part of this "first team," and the translator Wanda Boeke, who did an enormous amount of work in the organization of translations and acquisition of funds and copyright permissions. Erica Eijsker has also been a great fundraiser. I was blessed with an attentive and competent coeditor, Yopie Prins, who helped me to complete this manuscript. My assistant Agnes Andeweg and the translator Myra Scholz provided invaluable support at several stages. I am also indebted to Rudi Wester, Director of the Foundation for the Production and Translation of Dutch Literature. Finally I warmly thank all the poets and translators who have been willing to contribute to this collection with their work, their advice, and their indispensable enthusiasm.

Maaike Meijer
Amsterdam, The Netherlands
October 1997

The publisher gratefully acknowledges the financial support of the Foundation for the Production and Translation of Dutch Literature. We also thank the Prins Bernhard Fonds for their contribution.

INTRODUCTION

How many anthologies could be compiled from the collected works of women poets from the Low Countries? A great many, no doubt.[1] Large volumes could be filled with obedient women's poems, poems on nature, poems of religious or conjugal love, didactic poems, or poems for children. The focus of this collection, however, is specifically on feminist poetry. Defining the word *feminist* in a broad sense, we chose woman-identified works, poems with telling glimpses into women's lives, poems that resist mainstream heterosexual pressures and the social and erotic confinement that often accompany them. We gave priority to poets disenchanted with conventional romance as it was defined in their time. We looked for daring, autonomous, lusty, humorous, sassy poems, texts that strikingly portray women's dreams and fears and glories, and women's acts of writing. However debatable and ahistorical it may be to group all these poems together under the label "feminist," we gladly take the risks implied. As in the other volumes of the *Defiant Muse* series, the poems have been arranged chronologically. Reading them in that order will give a sense of the evolution of women's poetry in the Low Countries. If women can be said to have "a literature of their own"—as feminist scholars have claimed for the English tradition (Showalter 1977)—this is certainly true of Netherlandic poetry as well. In the following pages, I will trace some historical developments, paying special attention to the discontinuities with men's poetry, and to the coherence of women's poetry as a corpus in its own right.

Beginnings

The tradition of women's poetry in the Low Countries emerged long before the Dutch and Belgian nation states existed as we know them today. Its origins can be described best in terms of a wider, European context. Literary history, from this perspective, does not begin with the famous first *written* lines in the vernacular, but with the oral literatures of traditional agrarian societies. The important opening chapter of an anthology of women's poetry must therefore offer the love songs, work songs, lullabies, mourning songs, dance songs, ballads, stories, riddles, and fairytales that date back to a time long before writing became the primary tool for cultural transmission. Although most oral traditions have long been discarded, scholars in the past thirty years have begun studying the transition from orality to literacy (see Ong 1967; 1982), not only in Greek and Hebrew cultures of Antiquity, but also in European cultures of the Middle Ages. As in surviving traditional societies, two distinct spheres can be identified in medieval European cultures: one dominated by men and the other by women, based on the division of labor between the sexes. We can picture these two cultural worlds as equal but different, each sex having its own type of traditional knowledge, its own way of deal-ing with love, life, death, nature and religion, its own songs and literary gen-res, its own musical instruments and even its own ways of dancing and performing songs. . . . On the whole men's traditions developed along the line of the epic-narrative, . . . whereas the women created their genres along the line of the lyric-narrative. (Lemaire 1987a, 185–86)

Women's songs, such as the French *chansons de toile* or *chansons d'is-toire* and the oldest *malmariées,* the Portuguese *cantigas d'amigo,* the Spanish *jarchas,* the Castillian and Catalan *cantar de doncella,* and the German *Frauenlieder,* have found their way into many European song col-lections. These songs and poems reveal their oral origins through rhythm, repetition, assonance, and formulaic patterns. They often have a female lyrical subject, a female "I." They deal with longing for love, the meeting with the beloved, and the joy and grief that love brings. In these songs erot-ic relationships appear in a very different light from that of men's court-ly verse. Significantly, women are portrayed as actively seeking erotic encounters. The attitude toward sexuality is positive, accepting, and far removed from Christian fear and prudery (Lemaire 1987b). This explains, in part, why women's songs have been largely repressed in the literary canon: some were forbidden by the Church as "cantica turpia, obscoena et dia-bolica" ("shameful, obscene, and devilish songs"); others were rewritten as religious songs—*contrafactura,* as they were called.

Furthermore, in the absence of claimed authorship, it has been easy to attribute these songs to male authors. Some women's genres were, in fact, taken over by men and adapted to the male perspective on love and sex. In medieval song collections like the *Antwerps Liedboeck,* however, we find texts that are very likely original women's songs. We chose "Die nachte-gael die sanck een liedt" ("The nightingale sang a song") and the dawn poem or watchman's song "Den dach en wil niet verborghen sijn" ("The day will no more hidden be"), in which a woman bemoans the departure of her lover in the morning. The famous ballad "Het daghet inden oosten" ("The East's alight with dawning"), also a dawn poem, tells the story of a young woman who enters a nunnery after her lover is slain by a rival and her family deserts her. It belongs to the European genre of the "nun's song," and provides advice to young women on what to do if they should lose a lover. Tradition has it that this song was sung daily by a beguine, Gertrudis van Oosten, in Delft, in the first half of the fourteenth centu-ry. Her last name was said to derive from her frequent performances of "Het daghet inden oosten." At times she sang this song with two other women "on the bridges of the town and in other suitable places" (Alberdingk Thijm, ed. 1879, 56–72). The song might have had a special appeal for her, for according to legend, she herself took the veil after a great disappointment in love. Whether the story is true or not, the *vita sanctae* itself shows us a woman performing songs in public as a completely acceptable figure.[2]

Also remarkable is the medieval ballad "Heer Halewyn zong een liedekyn" ("Sir Halewin he sang a song")—of which numerous variants are known in England, Germany, and Scotland. This song relates the story of a heroic maiden who, by a clever ruse, manages to kill Halewin, slayer of women. Like many medieval songs, this one deals openly with brute sexual violence and the ways in which women could defend themselves against it. Songs, then, could be used by women as a medium for passing on their knowledge about the dangers of life to the next generation.

As literacy gradually spread over Europe, oral traditions did not immediately die out—some of them have, in fact, survived to the present day. We include "Anne Marieken," a lusty women's song recorded in the nineteenth century, and "De ploegtrekker" ("The Song of the Plow"), a testimony to folk customs that empowered women. The latter poem vividly describes how a man who beat his wife was punished by a community of women.

The High Middle Ages

Until the end of the fifteenth century all Netherlandic women poets that we know by name were beguines or nuns. Cloisters and religious communities were obviously the centers of culture, where writing was taught and preserved. Most remarkable are the works of Hadewijch (first half of the thirteenth century), who ranks among the great women mystics of the Middle Ages; Hildegard von Bingen (whose work Hadewijch mentions), Elisabeth von Schönau, Gertrud von Helfta, and Mechtild von Hackborn in Germany; and Catherina of Siena in Italy.

Hadewijch's breathtaking work consists of poems, "visions" written in prose, and letters. The letters show her to be a powerful personality, probably of noble origin, accustomed to ruling and giving advice. Very much her own woman, she never refers to herself as "a mere woman," never belittles her vocation, never shows any of the "feminine" modesty or restraint we know so well from women writers of later times. She is totally dedicated to her demanding and passionate inner life. Hadewijch's letters suggest that she was the spiritual leader of a group of beguines, women who had organized a large number of independent communities by the beginning of the thirteenth century. The practical and spiritual autonomy of her religious group might well account for Hadewijch's natural leadership and her freedom of thought and expression. Later in the century groups of this kind were increasingly brought under male and orthodox control, and incorporated into the regular monastic orders.

Hadewijch's all-pervading theme is *Minne* (Love) and how to deal with this great and at times terrible force that unites the soul with God. She often describes mystic union with God in highly physical terms. In her seventh vision a great eagle flies from the altar and announces God's arrival to her. God appears in the shape of a young man who first gives her communion, then embraces her:

he came to me in person. And he embraced me completely and pressed me against him, and with all my limbs I felt his body, as much as my human heart could desire. I was fully aware of being completely satisfied. I had the strength to bear that bliss for a short time. But very soon I lost the image of this splendid man. And I saw him diminish and evaporate and melt away, so that I could no longer see or perceive him outwardly, nor could I discern him in my inner self. Then it seemed to me as if we were one, without difference. I experienced all this with full awareness, as something seen, tasted and felt, as the sensuous tasting when one receives the sacrament, and as the physical seeing and feeling when a lover receives a lover into herself in a flood of blissful sights and sounds and the sense of losing oneself in the other. (Vekeman, ed. 1980, 96–98, transl. M. M.)

This undivided experience of physical and spiritual passion is a recurring motif among medieval religious writers. Hadewijch's spirituality is of a radical introversion, in the sense that it is exclusively directed toward the inner world. The individual soul is represented as the theater for the personal encounter with the Divine, Hadewijch's one and only subject.

A very different, and much more worldly spirituality appears in Anna Bijns. Bijns (1493–ca.1575) established herself as the first secular woman poet of the Netherlandic area. Neither nun nor beguine, she earned her living as an unmarried schoolteacher in Antwerp. Bijns was passionately involved in the religious politics of her day. Herself a Roman Catholic, she wrote many vehement poems against Luther and his followers. She shows great mastery of the *refrein,* the most important poetic form of the *rederijker* (rhetorician's) movement, in which she participated. The *refrein* is a long stanzaic poem, with the same line or *stockregel* ending each stanza. Especially powerful are Bijns's "sexual politics" poems, such as "Het waer goet houwen, maer tsorgen es de plage" ("Marriage would be fine if it weren't plagued with worry")—the one we include—and "Dweigeren staet den meiskens met allen wel" ("To refuse is very becoming for girls"), poems that can be seen as Bijns's answer to the increasing sixteenth-century propaganda to drive women back into the home. In 1985 Anna Bijns's name was given to the important Anna Bijns prize for women writers in the Dutch language.

The Renaissance

The Renaissance, with its sweeping cultural changes, fostered a new generation of women poets associated primarily with the fashionable secular literary circles of Amsterdam and The Hague: Anna Roemers Visscher (1584–1651), Maria Tesselschade Roemers Visscher (1594–1649), Katharina Questiers (1631–1669), Johanna Comans (?–1659), and Anna Maria van Schurman (1607–1678). Most of them were daughters or friends of famous male literary figures. This may well account for their opportunity to write at all, and it is probably the only reason that some of their work survived.

The sister poets Anna Roemers Visscher and Maria Tesselschade were daughters of the Amsterdam merchant, humanist, rhetorician, and Maecenas Roemer Visscher. Their house was a meeting place for the artistic elite of the day: Jacob Cats, Constantijn Huygens, Joost van den Vondel, Gerbrant Breero, Pieter Cornelisz Hooft, and many others. When Roemer Visscher died, in 1620, the circle moved to Hooft's residence, the castle of Muiden. This "Muiden Circle" can be envisaged as a lively and changing company of friends, all very privileged, powerful, witty, traveled, and educated according to the new Renaissance standards. They came together regularly to read one another's work, to discuss science and politics, to sing, to enjoy themselves, and to flirt. Innumerable letters and occasional verses were exchanged among the members of the circle.

The women in the group included the young wives of the already married men, Anna Roemers Visscher until her late marriage in 1624, her younger sister Maria Tesselschade, and Maria's friend, the singer Francisca Duarte. Maria Tesselschade is the one who emerges most vividly from letters and poems: always lovingly referred to as "Tesseltje," she is portrayed as a charming little bird, the frequently courted darling of the company. The Renaissance ideal of the male "uomo universale" found a female counterpart in these women. Anna Roemers spoke French and Italian, was an engraver of glass (then highly regarded as an art), she painted, embroidered, sang, played musical instruments, and worked as a poet and translator. Maria Tesselschade was skilled in all these arts as well. Katharina Questiers was a poet, engraver, painter, embroiderer, and translator. Such skills were typical of women writers at the time. The learned Margaretha Godewijck spoke several languages and studied sciences and philosophy. Anna Maria van Schurman was not only educated in the arts, but knew the modern languages (French, English, and German) as well as Latin, Greek, Hebrew, and other original languages of the Bible such as Chaldean, Syriac, Arabic, and Ethiopian. She also mastered the theology and the natural sciences of her day. (de Baar a.o. 1996).

The question, of course, is whether the Renaissance meant a cultural rebirth for women as well as for men. "Did women have a Renaissance?" as Joan Kelly (1984) put it, thus challenging Jacob Burckhardt's traditional, genderneutral picture of the Renaissance. Kelly questions whether women could participate in the vast new cultural possibilities that became available to (upper class) men at that time. The social and artistic lives of the women poets as I have sketched them so far seem to invite a positive answer to Kelly's question. Certainly, opportunities opened up for elite women that only a free noblewoman like Hadewijch had enjoyed before. On the other hand, women at this time became defensive about their writing. Comans's excuse for her verse, "Al wat ick maecken can en is maer vrouwenwerck" ("Whatever I can produce, it is but woman's work") is telling. The place of women in society came, during this and the next two centuries, more and more to be defined as a subordinate sphere, as women were barred from certain professions and crafts through new regulations of an expanding economy, and as the bourgeoisie streamlined its marriage practices, gradually controlling the legitimacy of its offspring and the virginity of brides. Printing brought in its wake not only the spread of knowledge, but also the widespread imposition of patriarchal bourgeois ideology (Spies 1985).

Furthermore, the problem with this new generation of secular Renaissance women poets is that they seem to owe their place in literary history to a self-perpetuating tradition of male praise. First they were excessively praised by contemporaries, later by a series of historiographers who often devoted more words to literally repeating what male contemporaries had said *about* these women writers than to discussing their work in an original or enlightening way. As for the contemporaries: Anna Roemers Visscher was highly praised by Vondel, Cats, Huygens, and others. They called her a second Sappho, a tenth Muse, a fourth Grace, the first virgin who climbed the Helicon, and more. The same panegyrics were showered upon Tesselschade[3]; Vondel and Breero dedicated works to her. Katharina Questiers, daughter of a poet, was extolled by Vondel, Huygens, Jan Vos, Joachim Oudaen, Joan Blasius. And Anna Maria van Schurman was the absolute celebrity of her time, marveled at and praised by almost everyone who wielded a pen. One might object, of course, that laudatory poems were an extremely common genre. It was simply one of the social and literary conventions of the time to express admiration for one another. But that does not account for the excess: men praised women more, and differently, than they did their fellow men. My impression is that the panegyrics constructed the women poets as miraculous sheep with five legs, as rare birds, as exceptions. An exceptional woman does not endanger normality. The effect of the praise was, in any case, that the women poets were safely enshrined and thus isolated from common womanhood.

Later historiographers say little of substance about the work of these Renaissance women poets; they tend instead merely to repeat other men's praise of them—their way, it seems, of invoking authority to justify a woman's presence in the canon. If Vondel, Breero, Huygens, and Cats said she was wonderful, then transhistorical intermale solidarity forbids that she be ignored. Men's praise for their fellow men is not repeated as emphatically by later generations of scholars; the presence of men in the canon does not require such justification.

Modern historiographers are even less inclined to mention women's praise of *one another.* Nobody tells us that Anna Roemers Visscher wrote poems for Georgette de Montenay (whose *Cent emblêmes chrestiens* she translated from the French), for Johanna Comans, Anna Maria van Schurman—all included in this collection—and for other women writers. Or that Ioanna Comans wrote a poem for her friend Anna. Or that Katharina Questiers, who had a maxim on her door, "Ick min mijn vrijheid" ("I love my freedom"), published the *Lauwerstryt* (*Praise Contest,* 1665) together with her bosom friend Cornelia van der Veer, in which they competed in writing laudatory poems addressed to each other. Just how wittily they played with the genre can be witnessed in Questiers's poem, included here, written on the occasion of finding van der Veer's garter in her room. These poems, it is true, belonged to a genre as popular in their time as poems on romantic friendship were in the eighteenth century. By writing such poems women might even have contributed to the construction of the woman writer as a rare bird, as an exception. However, the tone in which women practiced the genre also gives evidence of a network of female friendship and solidarity. Such networks are traceable in Netherlandic women's poetry—as in other European women's poetry—from the Renaissance to the early nineteenth century.

The Eighteenth Century: Humor, Learning, Romantic Friendship

From the period between 1650 and 1800 we could summon up a host of women poets, almost all of them completely forgotten today. With the exception of Elizabeth Maria Post and the duo Betje Wolff-Bekker and Aagje Deken, they have not been studied at all, and editions of their work, many of which appeared posthumously, are difficult to find.[4] Reappraisal of the eighteenth century would be rewarding, especially because of the many humorous poems found there. We include two matching poems—by Zara Maria van Zon (?–1755) and by Juliana Cornelia de Lannoy (1738–1782)—on the century's cherished topic, "inconstancy." Whereas van Zon composes her genre piece seriously, using the paradox "there is nothing constant but inconstancy," de Lannoy subverts it. Starting with the train of thought typical of the genre—All Great Things in the past have come to dust, and so will our material world—she then gives the poem an ironic twist by contrasting the pompous past with the homely present. The juxtaposition of the lofty and the low, the venerable and the all-too-common, is of course a classic humorous device.

Intriguing are the ways in which de Lannoy positions herself as outside the mainstream of poetic tradition. Her three volumes include many poems typical of the day: sonorous laudatory poems, occasional verses, poems celebrating national glory and great heroes, topical poems on religion, the home, nature. Unexpectedly, however, some poems crack the mask. Such is true of her hilarious satire on etiquette, "Het Gastmaal" ("The Banquet," 1777), and even more so of the poem "De Volmaakte Man" ("The Perfect Man"). The latter work—included in this collection—starts with the commonplace glorification of the husband as embodiment of male virtue: he works hard, fights for his country, never drinks, and loves his wife. De Lannoy pushes the genre to its extreme, and finally subverts it with her concluding line: "That man, doubly blessed to inspire my poem, / Has, so to see, never walked on this earth." She similarly ridicules works written in memory of great historic deeds. In the poem entitled "Lycaon," after the great general from Antiquity, she succeeds in building up her readers' expectations to a point of climax: Lycaon wields his invincible sword over his head, six . . . seven times . . .

"And . . . 'What did he do next?' In truth, I've forgotten." Thus de Lannoy lets the pompous poetry of her day capsize under its own weight. This almost modern, deconstructivist spirit of mockery can also be found in the long poem "Aan de Heeren Bestuurderen" ("To the Gentlemen of the Board"), written when she was elected an honorary member of the (exclusively male) Poetry Society of The Hague. Instead of effusing humble gratitude, de Lannoy keeps a guarded and ironic distance. She ends with the request that the gentlemen send her a list of their defects. Since she is most experienced in satirical writing, she is willing to compose satires on the shortcomings of the highly respected gentlemen who have admitted her to their noble ranks! This long poem can also serve as an example of the genre of pre-Enlightenment feminist polemic, which was often conducted in lengthy verse, and which women writers like Betje Wolff practiced as well.

Though we have already seen networks of friendship and admiration among women poets of the Renaissance,[5] special forms of "romantic friend-ship" came to flourish in the eighteenth and nineteenth centuries.[6] Betje Wolff-Bekker and Aagje Deken offer a prime example of women living out this ideal in the Low Countries. These Dutch "Ladies of Llangollen" found each other in 1776, when they were approaching their forties.[7] It was love at first sight. After the death of Betje's husband, the Reverend Wolff—his decease is the subject of Betje's moving poem to Aagje, included here—they decided to live together. Wolff-Bekker and Deken coauthored numerous novels, which are still highly readable today. They also formed the core of a lively network of learned, literary, and women-loving women. Both of them had already had several intimate relationships with women (Betje also with men) before they met. Aagje Deken's sen-timental friendships with Maria Bavinck and with the poet Maria Bosch are documented in the book of poems Aagje compiled of their joint works, *Stichtelijke gedichten van Maria Bosch en Agatha Deken* (*Devotional Poems by Maria Bosch and Agatha Deken*). The Deken-Bosch relationship characteristically mixes highly emotional "divine friendship" and pietist religiosity. Deken's poem "Vriendschapszucht" ("Love of Friendship"), includ-ed here, exemplifies this peculiar blend of feelings. Romantic friendship of the religious variety was generally accepted and valued at the time, cer-tainly among the middle and upper classes, as the profusion of devout and devoted poems exchanged between women shows. This public acclaim of intimate female—and male—same-sex friendship, which was deemed to be of great value for the formation of the soul and the refinement of the feelings, runs strikingly parallel to the pattern that Lillian Faderman (1981) has described in presexologist and pre-Freudian Anglo-American culture, in which romantic friendship was an "institution," a cultural ideal. Antifeminism and the intervention of the sexologists, with their inven-tion of the "perversions" alongside normative heterosexuality, would throw a very different light on these friendships from the mid-nineteenth century onward. They would become increasingly "suspect."

There were other distinct types of romantic friendship besides the religious variety (associated with Deken, Bosch, and Elisabeth Maria Post in the eighteenth-century, and with Petronella Moens and Adriana van Overstraten in the nineteenth century). Learned women cultivated special romantic attachments in which the erudition of the adored one was given erotic overtones. The life of the passionate Betje Wolff-Bekker is a series of such "learned amorousnesses." She adored the teacher of her adolescent years, Petronella Johanna de Timmerman, with whom she studied mathematics, astronomy, philosophy, and theology. This friendship effortlessly survived the later marriages of both women. While married to the older Reverend Wolff, Betje formed a passionate friendship with Anna van der Horst; they read the philosophers of the Enlightenment and brooded over feminist ideas.

Betje's long and moving poem "Aan mejuffer Anna van der Horst" (To Miss Anna van der Horst) could not be included in this volume for its length, but serves as an exemplary summary of what the learned romantic friendship was all about. The poem starts by praising Anna, "My van der Horst!," who is so skillful in "the useful arts and the illustrious sciences." But Anna is not the only woman who "reads and thinks, yes! who is mistress of wonder." To prove that she is not a lonely exception, Betje proudly mentions the great women of the seventeenth century: Barlaeus's daughter, Tesselschade, Anna Maria van Schurman, Katharyne Lescailje, and "lovely de With." She proceeds to list famous female contemporaries, and undertakes with Anna an imaginary journey to the "silent cell" of Betje's beloved teacher Petronella Johanna de Timmerman. On their travels they also encounter the women poets de Neufville and van Merken, as well as learned women of France: Madame Dacier, Madame de Lambert, Mademoiselle de Scudéry. The poem ends with an Ode to Friendship: friends will be united again after this life because friendship is eternal.

The self-awareness that marks Betje's journey with Anna through her female cultural heritage is extraordinary. She creates her own female literary tradition, takes personal possession of it, and at the same time lays it at Anna's feet. The poem is itself a gift of love. As such it unites women's love for each other with their poetic and learned endeavors. It projects a woman-identified universe, where such friendship has room to breathe.

Domna Stanton points to a strikingly similar phenomenon in French women's poetry of the time. The role of Muse can be filled by a woman, and "poems highlight lists of celebrated foremothers and contemporaries as objects of inspiration and veneration" (Stanton 1986, xxii). This suggests that Betje Wolff's "Aan mejuffer Anna van der Horst" is a specimen of topical verse that—among women—enjoyed international currency.

Modernity

I am skipping the greater part of the nineteenth century in this antholo-gy, since it is much more the age of the novel than an age of poetry. Important women novelists, such as Truitje Bosboom Toussaint, Margaretha Jacoba de Neufville, Elisabeth Johanna Hasebroek, and Elise van Calcar wrote few poems. The feminist revolution, gathering momentum in the last twen-ty years of the century, mainly unrolled in prose. But I included two poems by Wilhelmina Katharina Bilderdijk (1777–1830), wife of the famous poet Willem Bilderdijk. Her work was first published in 1858–1860, twenty-eight years after her death. Wilhelmina bore eight children, only one of whom survived, unfortunately not a rare set of circumstances then. She wrote some fifteen poems on these untimely deaths. The tone in the poem for the child Adelheide Irene, named after her two deceased sisters, is hardly desperate or enraged: the girl was the sixth child to die.

Equally remarkable is Petronella Moens (1777–1843), blind from her fourth year onward, but one of the most productive poets and writers of the early nineteenth century. With the lifelong help of a maid and a sec-retary, she could live off her pen. Her biography was written in 1872, by her close friend, the younger Flemish-born Maria van Ackere Doolaeghe (1803–1884), herself a successful poet. The two Flemish sisters Rosalie en Virginie Loveling, both very popular among the uneducated class, mark the second half of the nineteenth century.

The genealogy of women poets in the late nineteenth and twentieth cen-tury could be presented as a story of incompatibility, of the discontinu-ity between women's and men's poetry of the same period, for the work produced by women often seems to follow a course all its own.

Among the women poets who started writing at the end of the nineteenth century were Giza Ritschl (1869–1942), Henriette Roland Holst (1869–1952)—both included in this volume—Hélène Swarth (1859–1941), Jacqueline van der Waals (1868–1922), Nine van der Schaaf (1882–1973), and, somewhat later, Alice Nahon (1896–1933). Swarth and Nahon embody the enclosure of the female poet in the traditional realm assigned to women: they write about love, especially as the passively suffering victims of heterosexual romance (Swarth), and about nature and sentimentalized religion (Nahon). As women they lacked the solid education and background that could have saved them from the undifferentiated swamp of "feminine" feelings their poems drown in. Both of them worked during the heyday of first-wave fem-inism, which had a considerable impact on many women prose writers in Holland but not at all on these two poets. Swarth was adopted by the Tachtigers (the Eighties Poets, a late parallel to the English Romantics) as their token woman. The words in which the leaders of "Tachtig" charac-terize their new acquisition are telling. Van Deijssel is delighted that Swarth is "a woman who . . . gives herself to the people" (Van Deijssel 1897, 73-82). Willem Kloos writes, "[Swarth is] the singing heart in our litera-ture which gives itself to the world, naked in its glorious beauty and goodness, beautiful in its breathing, bleeding humanity" (Kloos n.d., 118). The metaphor of "giving herself" (for selling her poems, working as a poet) seems appropriate to these men for a woman, and Kloos almost sadistically projects this image onto Swarth: in his voyeuristic discourse she becomes a kind of bleeding female Christ. In this way Swarth herself, and the men who gratefully adopted her, created a new persona for the female poet generally. It was their solution to the problem women pose by the mere fact that they write, and by the defiance of the feminine such activity implies. The institution of poetry has always solved that problem by creating an acceptable image of the female poet. Nine van der Schaaf avoids this stereotype by showing a lively interest in social issues. And Giza Ritschl, originally Hungarian, writes intriguing poems about the dark side of love, full of revenge and doom. But the greatest of this generation is Henriette Roland Holst-van der Schalk (1869–1952).

To fully appreciate this most important female poet of the period, Roland Holst should be viewed against the backdrop not only of male poets of her time—the symbolists, the philosophical "generation of 1910," and her socialist comrade Herman Gorter—but of her female contemporaries as well. The swamp of undifferentiated "feminine" feeling threatened her, too, but she found her own way of escape. Through her work she struggled against everything that contemporaries like Hélène Swarth and Alice Nahon, represented: apolitical, badly educated, traditionally "feminine," passive, upper-middle-class writers, not involved in the world. Henriette Roland Holst educated herself systematically—reading Dante and Spinoza on the advice of fellow poet Gorter, struggling through Marx's *Das Kapital,* and perfecting her knowledge of French, German, Italian, and English languages and literatures. She taught herself Russian as she became a socialist and took an active part in the social and political life of her time. She left her safe upper-class milieu to become an independent woman and—eventually—an international socialist leader, a move portrayed as both a personal and poetic transformation in her powerful book *De nieuwe geboort* (*The New Birth,* 1902). Many poems in this volume, as in her later work, are deeply woman-identified and testify to a feminist conversion, though male historiographers have focused mainly on her conversion to socialism.

Typical of Henriette Roland Holst's "Bildungs" poems is the cycle *Gebroken kleuren I (Broken Colors).* There she describes in the first person the empty life of an upper-class girl ("I found my mind barren and empty") and her disappointment in the lives and thoughts of the women around her:

> they seemed to be swarming so timidly,
> blindly around just one thing;
> this looking, half bashful, half glad,
> this worry about the tiny and small,

a doll's game it seemed to me
and I thought: their souls are dying,
they don't know themselves who they are;
[. . .] and I called: "does this satisfy you?
there is still another existence."

The central character of the cycle then goes out into the world to work. After the first period of joy and exhilaration doubts begin to nag. She feels she is losing contact, through all her outward activity, with the receiving, feeling side of her character, as if "I were roaming on the outside of life." She dreams she has a child. She talks to many poor women, who tell her their life stories, and realizes the painful distance between them and herself.

But did I understand it all? There was
a veil between them and me,
a division I always saw.

She wonders: Do the proletarian women trust me? Are they jealous of my freedom, or am I jealous of their motherhood? Are they reticent for fear of hurting me? Why this mutual, guarded evasiveness? Why do both they and I have only half a life? "We avoided each other's deepest essence / through a common will." I know of no poem that has more subtly and honestly described the minefield of class differences between women.

This long, beautiful cycle deals with the depths of inward struggle, with the impossibility of returning to a traditional female life in the shadows, with the forging of a historically new woman's existence. The poems document the process of radical change that the *avant-garde* of women underwent collectively at the beginning of the century. This cycle breaks through the barriers among poetry, autobiography, feminist theory and political vision, as Adrienne Rich's poetry will do later, in the seventies.

Henriette Roland Holst's extensive oeuvre has not been given the scholarly attention it deserves. The same is true of the women poets who succeeded her. The number of critical studies on great women poets of the twentieth century, such as the Flemish Julia Tulkens and Christine D'haen, the South African Elisabeth Eybers, the Dutch M. Vasalis, Ida Gerhardt, and Ellen Warmond, is extremely small compared to the number devoted to their male colleagues. I believe this lack of critical attention is related to the in-between position women poets occupy in literary history. The case of Henriette Roland Holst can be taken as paradigmatic. On the one hand she belongs to the poetic tradition shaped by men: she is an heir to symbolism, a transformer—with Herman Gorter—of socialist and communist ideas into poetry, a writer clearly indebted to classic philosophers such as Spinoza, Dante, More, and Erasmus. But analysis of her work as part of mainstream tradition reduces it by obscuring woman-identified parts and ignoring its feminist essence. To see her as a "loner" does her no justice either. What we need is a multiple perspective on Roland Holst, one which could describe her use of symbolist imagery in the context of her particular socialist-feminist vision; and which could acknowledge the fact that she only *in part* belonged to the literary and political culture dominated by men. Throughout her work Roland Holst often expresses the angry fear of not being totally accepted by the "brotherhood" of left-wing men. Also, her creative involvement with Dante—in *De vrouw in het woud* (*The Woman in the Forest*, 1912)—is an illuminating case of what Alicia Ostriker (1982) has called "revisionist mythmaking." This book of poems was written after a traumatic breakup in the socialist party, and Roland Holst intertextually reworked Dante's wandering in the "selva oscura" (*Inferno* 1, 2). Such a multiple perspective would bring to light the contrasts with her female contemporaries as well, showing how she breaks down the old and new patriarchal constructions of what a woman poet should be and what she should write about. And, finally, it would allow for appreciation of her innovative role within the dominant tradition. Her *Bildungs* poems, for example, are sometimes written in free verse, sometimes with a fresh and idiosyncratic use of the old forms. Both poetic styles were remarkably advanced for the time. It is as if Roland Holst were transforming worn-out poetic forms together with the worn-out shadow life of women.[8]

The Encompassing Vision

We need the same sort of multiple perspective to assess the most important poets of the next generation: Elisabeth Eybers (1915–), M. Vasalis (1909–), Ida Gerhardt (1905–1997) and the younger, Belgian, Christine D'haen (1923–), who published their first books in 1936, 1940, 1945, and 1951 respectively. All four have ties to the dominant tradition, yet are not completely at home there. Eybers's move from South Africa to Holland in 1961 set her on an individual literary course. Vasalis, Gerhardt, and D'haen worked very much on their own; having little connection to journals and groups, they were especially critical of the "Vijftigers," the experimental poets who came to power in the early fifties. While these "angry young men" aggressively proclaimed themselves the makers of a new poetry, and were canonized as such, Vasalis, Gerhardt, and D'haen remained aloof from this male poetic revolution. Thematically and technically they steered their own course. Yet the term "loner" is as inappropriate for them as for Henriette Roland Holst.

If I were writing literary history I would group Eybers, Vasalis, Gerhardt, and D'haen together as the poets of The Encompassing Vision. All of them write with a certain metaphysical breadth; a poetic "religion" or mythology pervades their work. Explicitly and without reticence they address the great problems of life: death, separation, great love, human destiny, and deep, often mystical experiences in nature. Their universe still forms a cohesive, meaningful whole, with the sacred dimensions of life often visible in everyday existence. Themes and metaphors, especially in Vasalis's, Eybers's and D'haen's work, are drawn from the sphere of women's experience. Vasalis and Eybers in particular use an unsensational, almost invisible technique; they are clearly not interested in producing poetry for poetry's sake.

Gerhardt and D'haen are more classical in their themes and forms, deliberately seeking continuity with the tradition. Both have produced cycles of woman-identified poems dealing with spiritual transformation. This suggests a close poetic affinity with Henriette Roland Holst.

The poets of The Encompassing Vision—now in their seventies and eighties—are in many ways the "Grand Old Ladies" of modern Dutch women's poetry. They are the first poets since Betje Wolff, of the eighteenth century, to show an awareness of a female literary tradition. Henriette Roland Holst, despite her revolutionary role, gives no evidence of this particular awareness. Gerhardt's work contains many references to Sappho as the archetypal woman poet. In addition, she wrote a poem for Henriette Roland Holst, and one for M. Vasalis, thus acknowledging a form of poetic sisterhood. She also greatly influenced the leading younger lesbian poet, Elly de Waard. Eybers wrote poems on Emily Dickinson, as well as one entitled "Brontë, Dickinson & Kie" ("Brontë, Dickinson & Co"), thus inscribing herself in the tradition she wishes to claim as her own. Vasalis has deeply influenced almost every woman poet after her, some of whom incorporate literal quotations from her work. Her voice and stance echo through many women's poems up to the present day.

Of the same generation as the poets of The Encompassing Vision are Clara Eggink (1906–1991), self-styled bohemian and one of the most colorful figures in Dutch literature from the twenties through the fifties; Anna Blaman (1905–60), whose early love poems to women initiated the tradition of Dutch lesbian poetry, still thriving today; the famous prose writer Hella Haasse; and Annie M. G. Schmidt (1911–1995), prolific writer of songs, musicals, poems, and children's books, whose subversive humor equals that of the eighteenth-century Juliana de Lannoy.

The Great Melancholy

The poets of The Encompassing Vision, Gerhardt, Eybers, Vasalis, and D'haen, can be clearly distinguished from their younger female contemporaries who started writing in the fifties. The women poets of this decade lost contact with the spiritual dimension and wrote bare, modernist, and often extremely depressed poetry. They had no ties with the male movement of the experimental "Vijftigers," although historiographers sometimes force the connection. Groping for a category to account for hundreds of poems by women that have no parallel in men's poetry of the time, I have introduced the term The Great Melancholy (Meijer 1987). Life is seen as useless; there is no interest in the outside world, or in other people. Unable to achieve anything, the persona tends to despise and blame herself for her worthlessness. The work of Ellen Warmond (1930–) and Hanny Michaelis

(1922–) is completely dominated by this theme. Nel Noordzij and the early Ankie Peypers are also touched by this prevailing dark mood.

Characteristic is "Changement de decor" (Change of Scene) by Ellen Warmond, in which a new day is experienced as an execution, and the loss of unity and sense takes on cosmic, apocalyptic proportions: stars fall from their fixed course. The persona is imprisoned in cold, unbearable terror.

> As soon as the day is shoved
> Like blackmail under my door,
> The red seals of dreams are cut
> By swift sunlight knives.
>
> Wearily houses open their bitter eyes,
> And stars fall pallid from their course.
>
> When the silent sentinels
> Nightdream and daydream
> Hastily trade places,
> The firing squad of the twelve
> New hours quietly takes aim.[9]

On a sociological level one can see a connection between The Great Melancholy and the general alienating situation of women in the fifties. It was a time of restoration, not only of bombed cities, but also of the family and the traditional role of women. Motherhood was held up as the only ideal, very few women had jobs, and the cultural representation of women was minimal. From a woman's point of view The Great Melancholy could be analyzed as a countermovement challenging the false optimism and the sexism of this restoration. Women poets state bluntly that life is unlivable and empty to them. The rebuilt cities they describe as prisons. Women are recommended as homemakers, but the four walls of the house, they say, close in on them. Women are supposed to be warm and feeling, but they claim not to feel at all. Women, expected to find their destiny in heterosexual love, show how powerless lovers are to stop the flood of depression. All this can be read as a rejection of that restoration. Strikingly, women poets from other European countries appear to have suffered the same collective loss of self, as they were writing similarly desperate poems at the time (Cocalis 1986, xix–xx).

However, The Great Melancholy invoked its own antipode in the same decade. Poets like Nel Noordzij (1923–) and Ankie Peypers (1928–) managed to write themselves out of initial depression into (pre)feminist discomfort, even revolt. I see The Great Melancholy and prefeminist dissatisfaction as two sides of the same coin. They symbolically represent and oppose the same set of impediments. Most interesting and enduring is the work of Ankie Peypers, which forms an illuminating link between the melancholy of the fifties and the new feminist and woman-identified poetry of the eighties and nineties. In "Huwelijk" ("Marriage"), written in

1951, two years after the publication of *Le deuxième sexe (The Second Sex)*, Peypers was already depicting marriage as claustrophobic, as the violent bumping into each other of man and wife, as the annihilation of the woman.

> My husband roams the room.
> It is small. We no longer try
> to avoid the other body.
>
> But every touch is like a hammer—
> blow so short and fierce—more and more afraid
> I do my duty to resemble him.[10]

The first organized group of women poets, The New Savages (1987–), aptly nominated Peypers as "Honorary Savage" during their reading tours of the late eighties.

Toward the End of the Century

In the sixties a similar discontinuity between Netherlandic men's and women's poetry is apparent, though the tables are turning. Men's poetry, which had been full of wild experiment, aggression, emotion, and poetic body language, cools down in the sixties. It becomes more distanced, impersonal, and ironic. Displaying personal emotion is increasingly "not done." There is a small revival of dadaism, and "ready-mades" (trivial text fragments, found on jam jars, in newspapers, or elsewhere in everyday life, reprinted in the form of poems) are popular. While the men sober up, women climb out of their "Great Melancholy" and exhibit great poetic vitality. The intimate, emotional, and personal—all the more effective since this generation of women poets deliberately shuns big words—dominates their work. With the metaphysical framework of the poets of The Encompassing Vision gone forever, they still perceive traces of transcendence and try—modestly, implicitly—to articulate meaning in life. Judith Herzberg (1934–) writes a subtle, sensuous poetry, where the small and seemingly insignificant always emerges as strange, confusing, full of wonder. Fritzi Harmsen van Beek (1927–) made her debut with sublime, baroque poetry filled with a desperately comic sadness. Neeltje Maria Min (1944–) is probably the most widely read woman poet of the Netherlands; her volume *Voor wie ik liefheb wil ik heten (For those I love I want to have a name),* with its direct, emotional, woman-identified poetry, sold 70,000 copies. In 1986, after a silence of twenty years, she published her second book, *Een vrouw bezoeken (To Visit a Woman),* which solves many of the mysteries lurking behind *Voor wie ik liefheb,* by presenting more explicit images of sexual violence.[11]

In the seventies, eighties, and nineties the house of women poets becomes too crowded for description by means of the simple, chronological narrative I have adopted so far. Regular references to the parallel story of men's poetry to illustrate the double bind of women poets are no longer enough, for one must now tell a story of triple binds, of multiplicity, and of multiculturalism.

The last links in my chain of chronology are some items of literary-sociological information. In 1985 an influential group of Dutch women writers called into existence the Anna Bijns Prize, named after the sixteenth-century poet mentioned earlier in this introduction. The prize (10,000 guilders), intended as the women's equivalent of the prestigious P. C. Hooft Prize (comparable to the British Booker Prize), is awarded every two years to a writer who represents "the female voice in literature." In 1987 Ellen Warmond received the Anna Bijns Prize for poetry; in 1993 Christine D'haen; in 1995 Hanny Michaelis. They are all represented in this volume. At the same time a group of young women poets, under the guidance of Elly de Waard, worked together regularly in reading and training sessions. They published the joint anthology *De Nieuwe Wilden (The New Savages)* (de Waard 1987) and presented themselves as the first group of women ever to organize themselves within the institution of poetry. These events are of course directly related to the feminist cultural institutions Dutch women have been building over the past twenty years: women's bookshops, book fairs, publishing houses, poetry festivals, feminist literary journals, and academic women's studies programs, all of which have helped to create an atmosphere in which women's literature can be produced, valued, discussed, and interpreted. This anthology is itself part of the countermovement. The controversies about such enterprises, which still rage in The Netherlands and Flanders, are reflected by the refusal of some poets to permit their work to be printed in this book. For this reason poems by M. Vasalis and Eva Gerlach are not found in these pages, a fact that the editors deeply regret.

A House with Many Rooms

We could envision the last twenty-five years of women's poetry as a multilayered structure of distinct but coexisting traditions, or as a set of overlapping and intersecting literary circles. In this anthology we have tried to do justice to the multiple nature of contemporary women's poetry. The reader will therefore find heterosexual and lesbian poetry, black, immigrant, and white poetry, Jewish and non-Jewish, classic and punk poetry here— all shaped, or at least tinged, by the social and cultural contexts from which they emerge. Without raising complex theoretical questions, we can safely assert that no poem passively reflects its setting, but is itself a reading, an interpretation. Every good poem conducts a dialogue with its context.

Netherlandic poetry is partly rooted in colonial history. As a result it is neither confined to the national borders of The Netherlands and Belgium, nor to the indigenous white population possessing Dutch and Belgian nationality. As imperialist and colonizing nations, the Low Countries exported Dutch as a language of domination to Surinam (Dutch Guiana), the Antilles, New Guinea, Indonesia, and South Africa. "Apartheid" is not only a system of racial oppression erected by the descendants of Dutch colonizers; it is also a Dutch word. While adopting a critical attitude toward white South African literature in Afrikaans (still read in Holland) with regard to its racial prejudice and flagrant, deeply rooted lack of commitment (Meijer 1988, 204–39), we have nevertheless included poems by the South African–born Elisabeth Eybers, one of the poets of The Encompassing Vision. After emigrating to Holland in 1961, Eybers continued to write in her mother tongue, Afrikaans. Consistently, however, she offers a critical reading of the context that the language brings into the poem. Each of her later volumes contains one or more poems in which she explicitly takes a stand against Apartheid, thus putting her political signature on the book as a whole. Eybers succeeded in transforming the "Pitbull Terrier" language of Afrikaans—the image we get from television—into a medium for expressing tenderness, doubt, and spiritual transformation (Otten 1987).

The people of Surinam and the Antilles, educated for generations in the Dutch language, have started producing Dutch literature of their own. Astrid Roemer (1947–) writes baroque, romantic, deliberately overstated verse, full of allusions to other black texts, both literary and nonliterary. She often includes poems in Sranantongo, now recognized as the standard language of Surinam. Since Sranan was thoroughly despised during the long history of Dutch cultural domination, Roemer's Sranan poems can be seen as a gesture of independence from oppressive colonial values. This poetry celebrates undomesticated, revindicated blackness.

Influences from the opposite end of the Dutch colonial world are found in Loes Nobel's (1931–) "Wangsalans," which draw on old Indonesian traditions of work songs. Other immigrants are also represented. Writing in Dutch and working in the Low Countries are several poets of Eastern European origin. We have included poems by Maja Panajotova (1951–) from Bulgaria and by Giza Ritschl (1869–1942) and Erika Dedinszky (1942–) from Hungary.

For many women poets Jewish history and postwar Jewish consciousness play a significant role. This preoccupation can be found in poems by Hanny Michaelis (1922–), Judith Herzberg (1934–), Sonja Pos (1936–), and Andreas Burnier (1931–), although their work should never be reduced to this one theme. That a poem has many intertwining voices is beautifully demonstrated in Burnier's poem "Op zoek naar Gertrude Stein" ("Looking for Gertrude Stein"). The lyrical "I," visiting the rue de Fleurus in Paris, remembers Stein as her forefather/mother, thus situating herself within a lesbian women's tradition—a tradition that she, through Stein, both criticizes and loves. Stein is remembered as a Jew, as a closeted lesbian, as a transsexual. By giving Stein the epithet "Caesar of the turning century," the poet creates a persona which fulfills Stein's wishful fantasy of being reincarnated as a man. The speaker's loneliness, central to the poem, is a double one. It is a woman's loneliness—evoked by the sight of long lines of people waiting to see an exhibition of paintings by Gertrude's friend, Picasso. It is also a Jewish loneliness, evoked by the image of Stein in the "heaven of the Goyim," the diaspora. She continues to live in a strange "goyim" world, even after death. This deeply melancholic poem exemplifies the way in which a multiplicity of voices contributes to a poem's dialogue with contexts and traditions.

Finally, lesbian poetry can be studied as a distinct voice in modern Dutch women's poetry. This tradition starts with the explicitly lesbian poems of Anna Blaman (1905–1960), some written as early as 1939, in which she wrestled to overcome the tragic sense of monstrosity and doom surrounding lesbianism at the time. Most important today is Elly de Waard (1940–), who writes a technically superb neoclassical poetry, celebrating lesbian existence in all its dimensions. Also representative of this strand are the ironic neoromantic cult poems of Sjuul Deckwitz (1952–). And half of The New Savages write as if nothing were more "natural" than lesbian-voiced poems.

Women's poetry, in all its historical and regional diversity, presents itself today as a crossroads of cultures, a complex of intersecting fields, a composition of worlds. This anthology opens significant vistas into those worlds. May this book be a source of inspiration to all women and men, who are reading and writing poetry in Flemish and in Dutch. May all poetry readers and writers cherish this book as a precious gift our history has to offer. I especially hope that the women poets among us—whatever their class, religion, sexuality, and ethnicity—feel strenghtened by the knowledge of their foremothers: the great Hadewijch, the indomitable Anna Bijns, the jocular and yet wise Annie Schmidt, and the formidable Ida Gerhardt. And the remarkable anonymous poet, the unknown singer who composed the ballad of Sir Halewin, in which the clever princess beheads the slayer of women. This book is dedicated to all living Dutch and Flemish women poets. May they be able to behead and slay the shadows of self-doubt, the fear of misrepresentation and misreading, like true princesses. Now let the poems speak.

Maaike Meijer
Amsterdam, The Netherlands
October 1997

Notes to the Introduction

1. Interesting volumes in English of (contemporary) Dutch poetry by women were edited by Maria Jacobs (1985) and Manfred Wolf (1974). The collections edited by Joldersma (1990) and Aercke (1994) also include some poets, although most of the authors are prose writers.

2. It is amusing that in the case of Gertrudis van Oosten historiographers *invented* a poet, whereas the more usual practice has been to remain sweepingly oblivious of existing women poets. Gertrudis is mentioned in several historical sources: her life as a saint can be found in Bollandus's Acta *Sanctorum* (1643); a separately printed version of Gertrudis's life dates from 1589; and a document in the archives of Delft states that a Trude van Oosten, beguine, inherited one pound in 1349. Van Buuren (1988) collected all the evidence and concludes that Geertruyd's connection with the famous dawn poem is probably a legend. Nevertheless Jan Frans Willems's (1848) portrayal of her as a performing woman poet has been repeated by Alberdingk Thijm (1879), Lya Berger (1922, 77) and many other literary historiographers.

3. An illuminating new biography of Tesselschade is Mieke B. Smits-Veldt, *Maria Tesselschade: Leven met talent en vriendschap*. The first annotated edition of Tesselschade's own poems was also published in 1994: Agnes A. Sneller and Olga van Marion, eds., *De gedichten van Tesselschade Roemers*. These books replace J. A. Worp, *Een onwaerdeerlijcke vrouw* (1918), who intersperses Tesselschade's own writings with biographical information, letters addressed to her, letters to others about her, and a great many poems on her. Thus he presents Tesselschade as the walking Muse and predominantly as a function of male social relations.

4. The record is beginning to be set straight in an ambitious research project under the direction of Riet Schenkeveld-van der Dussen, who edited a nine-hundred-page Dutch anthology from the unpublished or out-of-print works of Dutch and Flemish women poets from 1550 to 1850, *Met en Zonder lauwerkrans*. With a team of scholars (Karel Porteman, Lia van Gemert, and Piet Couttenier), Schenkeveld produced a true encyclopedia of early Renaissance through mid-nineteenth-century women writers. Nine volumes of important texts by women writers from the same period, as well as a volume of scholarly essays on these writers, is scheduled to follow publication of the encyclopedia.

5. In the seventeenth century Titia Brongersma and Katharyne Lescailje also wrote on intense friendships with women.

6. Feminist scholars have beautifully documented romantic friendship as literary form and as lived reality in the Anglo-American world (Faderman 1981, Mavor 1973, Cott 1978); in France (Bonnet 1981); and in Germany (Schwarz 1983; also Kluckhohn 1966). For The Netherlands see Meijer (1983) and Everard (1994).

7. The "Ladies of Llangollen," Lady Eleanor Butler and Miss Sarah Ponsonby, formed a famous and fashionable English same-sex couple. They eloped in 1778 and settled in Llangollen in Wales, where they created a living legend. They were widely admired as writers, poets, and romantic friends. See Mavor (1973) for a biography.

8. A succinct overview in English of Henriette Roland Holst's life and work was provided by Johanna C. (Anneke) Prins in Joldersma (1990, 43–45). A beautiful Dutch biography of Henriette Roland Holst was recently published by Elsbeth Etty (1996).

9. Translated by Manfred Wolf in *The Shapes of Houses* (1974).

10. "Huwelijk" from Peypers (1976, 12). Translation by Maaike Meijer and Mary Wings in Meijer (1987, 168).

11. See my analysis of Min's work in chapters 4 and 5 of Meijer 1988.

Works Cited

Aercke, Kristiaan, ed. *Women Writing in Dutch*. Women Writers of the World, vol. 1. New York and London: Garland Publishing, 1994.

Alberdingk Thijm, Jos. Alb., ed. *Verspreide verhalen in proza*. Amsterdam: Van Langenhuysen, 1879.

Baar, M. de, et al. *Chosing the better part. Anna Maria van Schuurman (1607–1678)*. International Archives of the History of Ideas, 146. Dordrecht/Boston/London: Kluwer Academic Publishers, 1996.

Berger, Lya. *Les femmes Poètes de la Hollande*. Paris: Perrin, 1922.

Bollandus, Ioannes, ed. *Acta Sanctorum*. Antwerp, 1643.

Bonnet, Marie-Jo. *Un choix sans Equivoque. Recherches Historiques sur les Relations amoureuses entre les femmes XVIe–XXe siècle*. Paris: Denoël, 1981.

Buuren, A. M. J. van. "Geertruyd van Oosten and 'Het daget in den oosten.'" *Essays in Honour of Peter King*. Ed. Michael Wintle. London: Athlone Press. 75–87, 1988.

Cocalis, Susan, ed. *The Defiant Muse: German Feminist Poems from the Middle Ages to the Present*. A Bilingual Anthology. New York: The Feminist Press, 1986.

Cott, Nancy. "Passionlessness: An Interpretation of Victorian Sexual Ideology, 1790–1850." *Signs* 4 (1978): 219–236.

Deijssel, L. van. *Verzamelde opstellen 2*. Amsterdam, 1897.

Etty, Elsbeth. *Liefde is heel het leven niet. Henriette Roland Holst 1869–1952*. Amsterdam: Balans, 1996.

Everard, Myriam. *Ziel en zinnen: Over liefde en lust tussen vrouwen in de tweede helft van de achttiende eeuw*. Groningen: Historische Uitgeverij, 1994.

Faderman, Lillian. *Surpassing the Love of Men*. London: Junction Books, 1981.

Jacobs, Maria, ed. *With Other Words: A Bilingual Anthology of Contemporary Dutch Poetry by Women*. Windsor: Netherlandic Press, 1985.

Joldersma, Hermina, ed. *Women Writers in the Netherlands and Flanders*. Special issue of *Canadian Journal of Netherlandic Studies* XI, no. 2 (1990).

Kelly, Joan. "Did Women Have a Renaissance?" *Women, History and Theory*. Chicago: University of Chicago Press. 19–50, 1984.

Kloos, Willem. *Veertien jaar Literatuurgeschiedenis II*. Amsterdam, n.d.

Kluckhohn, Paul. *Die Auffassung der Liebe in der Literatur des 18. Jahrhunderts und in der Deutschen Romantik*. Tübingen: Niemeyer, 1966.

Lemaire, Ria. "Rethinking Literary History." *Historiography of Women's Cultural Traditions*. Ed. Maaike Meijer and Jetty Schaap. Dordrecht: Foris, 1987.

———. *Passions et positions. Contribution à une sémiotique du sujet dans la poésie lyrique médiévale en langues romanes*. Amsterdam: Rodopi, 1987b.

Mavor, Elizabeth. *The Ladies of Llangollen: A Study of Romantic Friendship.* Harmondsworth: Penguin Books, 1973.

Meijer, Maaike. "Pious and learned female bosom friends in Holland in the eighteenth century." *Among Men, Among Women: Sociological and Historical Recognition of Homosocial Arrangements.* Ed. M. Duyvis et al. Papers of the Gay Studies and Women's Studies Conference. Amsterdam: University of Amsterdam, 1983.

————. "The Great Melancholy: Notes Toward a History of Dutch Women's Poetry." *Historiography of Women's Cultural Traditions.* Ed. Maaike Meijer and Jetty Schaap. Dordrecht: Foris, 1987.

————. *De lust tot lezen. Nederlandse dichteressen en het literaire systeem.* Amsterdam: Van Gennep, 1988.

Meijer, Maaike, and Jetty Schaap, eds. *Historiography of Women's Cultural Traditions.* Dordrecht: Foris, 1987.

Ong, W. J. *The Presence of the Word.* New Haven: Yale University Press, 1967.

————. *Orality and Literacy: The Technologizing of the Word.* London: Methuen, 1982.

Ostriker, Alicia. "The Thieves of Language: Women Poets and Revisionist Mythmaking." *Signs* (Autumn 1982): 69–89.

Otten, Willem Jan. 1987. "De onverzoenlijke liefde: Poëzie van Elisabeth Eybers." *NRC*, 13 March 1987.

Peypers, Ankie. *Vezamelde gedichten.* Amsterdam: Bert Bakker, 1976.

Schenkeveld-van der Dussen, Riet, ed. *Met en zonder lauwerkrans. Schrijvende vrouwen uit de vroeg-moderne tijd 1550–1850, van Anna Bijns tot Elise van Calcar.* Amsterdam: Amsterdam University Press, 1997.

Schwarz, Gudrun. "Women Support Networks in Germany at the End of the 19th and Beginning of the 20th Century." *Among Men, Among Women: Sociological and Historical Recognition of Homosocial Arrangements.* Ed. M. Duyves et al. Papers of the Gay Studies and Women's Studies Conference. Amsterdam: University of Amsterdam, 1983.

Showalter, Elaine. *A Literature of Their Own.* Princeton, NJ: Princeton University Press, 1976.

Smits-Veldt, Mieke B. *Maria Tesselschade: Leven met talent en vriendschap.* Zutphen: Walburg Pers, 1994.

Sneller, Agnes A., and Olga van Marion, eds. *De gedichten van Tesselschade Roemers.* Hilversum: Verloren, 1994.

Spies, Marijke. *Des Mensen op- en nedergang: Literatuur en leven in de noordelijke Nederlanden in de zeventiende eeuw.* Bulkboek 148. Barneveld: Knippenberg, 1985.

Stanton, Domna C., ed. *The Defiant Muse: French Feminist Poems from the Middle Ages to the Present.* New York: The Feminist Press, 1986.

Vekeman, H. W. J., ed. *Het visioenenboek van Hadewijch.* Nijmegen: Dekker & van de Vegt, 1980.

Waard, Elly de. *Anna Bijns: O god wat hooren wij nu al Rumoers.* Amsterdam: Anna Bijns Stichting, 1985.

————, ed. *De nieuwe wilden in de poëzie.* Amsterdam: Sara, 1987.

Willems, Jan Frans. *Oude Vlaemsche Liederen.* Ghent, 1848.

Wolf, Manfred, ed. *The Shape of Houses: Women's Voices from Holland and Flanders.* Berkeley: Two Windows Press, 1974.

Worp, J. A. *Een onwaerdeerlycke Vrouw: Brieven en Verzen van en aan Maria Tesselschade.* Den Haag: Nijhoff, 1918.

[HEER HALEWYN ZONG EEN LIEDEKYN]

Heer Halewyn zong een liedekyn;
Al die dat hoorde, wou by hem zyn.

En dat vernam een koningskind,
Die was zoo schoon en zoo bemind.

Zy ging voor haren vader staen:
"Och vader, mag ik naer Halewyn gaen?"

"Och neen, gy dochter, neen, gy niet,
Die derwaert gaen, en keeren niet!"

Zy ging voor hare moeder staen:
"Och moeder, mag ik naer Halewyn gaen?"

"Och neen, gy dochter, neen, gy niet,
Die derwaert gaen, en keeren niet!"

Zy ging voor hare zuster staen:
"Och zuster, mag ik naer Halewyn gaen?"

"Och neen, gy zuster, neen, gy niet,
Die derwaert gaen, en keeren niet!"

Zy ging voor haren broeder staen:
"Och broeder, mag ik naer Halewyn gaen?"

"'t Is my al eens, waer dat gy gaet,
Als gy uw eer maer wel bewaerd
En gy uw kroon naer rechten draegt!"

Toen is zy op haer kamer gegaen
En deed haer beste kleeren aen.

Wat deed zy aen haren lyve?
Een hemdeken fynder als zyde.

Wat deed zy aen? Haer schoon korslyf:
Van gouden banden stond het styf.

Wat deed zy aen? Haren rooden rok:
Van steke tot steke een gouden knop.

[SIR HALEWIN HE SANG A SONG]*

Sir Halewin he sang a song.
All who heard him were lured along.

A king's daughter heard him call.
She was beautiful and loved by all.

She stood before her father: "Oh,
Father, to Halewin let me go."

"Oh no, my daughter, stay indoor,
Those who go thither are seen no more."

She stood before her mother: "Oh,
Mother, to Halewin let me go."

"Oh no, my daughter, stay indoor,
Those who go thither are seen no more."

She stood before her sister: "Oh,
Sister, to Halewin let me go."

"Oh no, my sister, stay indoor,
Those who go thither are seen no more."

She stood before her brother: "Oh,
Brother, to Halewin let me go."

"Go where thee liketh, what do I care.
But wear thy crown upon thine hair."

She went to her room, unlocked her chest,
And dressed herself in her Sunday best.

What did she put upon her skin?
A shirt of the finest silk they spin.

What did she put on her bodice fine?
Stiff it stood with golden twine.

What did she put on her red robe?
From stitch to stitch a golden knob.

---

* The translator has chosen to render the poem in regular two-line stanzas, thus "normalizing" the exceptional three-line stanzas in the source-text. The content, however, has not suffered as a result.

Wat deed zy aen? Haren keirle:
Van steke tot steke een peirle.

Wat deed zy aen haer schoon blond hair?
Een krone van goud en die woog zwaer.

Zy ging al in haers vaders stal
En koos daer 't besten ros van al.

Zy zette haer schrylings op het ros:
Al zingend en klingend reed zy doort bosch.

Als sy te midden 't bosch mogt zyn,
Daer vond zy myn heer Halewyn.

Hy bondt sijn peerd aen eenen boom,
De joncvrouw was vol anxt en schroom.

"Gegroet," sei hy, "gy schoone maegd,
Gegroet," sei hy, "bruyn oogen claer,
Comt, sit hier neer, ombindt u hair."

Soo menich hair dat si ombondt,
Soo menich traentjen haer ontron.

Zy reden met malkander voort
En op den weg viel menig woort.

Zy kwamen by een galgenveld,
Daer hing daeraen menich vrouwenbeeld.

Alsdan heeft hy tot haer gezeid:
"Mits gy de schoonste maget zyt,
Zoo kiest uw dood, het is nog tyd!"

"Wel, als ik dan hier kiezen zal,
Zoo kieze ik dan het zweerd voor al.

Maer trekt eerst uit uw opperst kleed,
Want maegdenbloed dat spreidt zoo breed:
Zoot u bespreide, het ware my leed!"

Eer dat zyn kleed getogen was,
Zyn hoofd lag voor zyn voeten ras,
Zyn tong nog deze woorden sprak:

"Gaet ginder in het koren
En blaest daer op myn horen,
Dat al myn vrienden 't hooren!"

What did she put on her mantelet?
From stitch to stitch a pearl was set.

What did she put on her soft blonde hair?
A crown of gold, none heavier.

She is to her father's stable gone,
And chose there his bravest stallion.

She mounted astride upon the steed
And singing and ringing rode through the glade.

When she was gone halfway the wood
She came to where Sir Halewin stood.

He bound his horse to a tree trunk,
The damsel trembled more and shrunk.

Said he: "I greet thee, beautiful maid,
Sit down by me, unbind thy braid."

So many a tress the maid untied.
So many a tear the maiden cried.

They rode together across the glade
And many a word fell by the way.

They are unto a gallows come.
Many a woman hung therefrom.

"Because thou art the loveliest maid,
Choose how thee liketh to die," he said.

"Since thou wilt give me choice of death,
I choose the sword," she answereth.

"But first take off thy coat and sash,
For maiden blood will spout and splash."

But ere Sir Halewin could doff
His coat and sash, his head was off.

And while it lay there at his feet,
His tongue said: "Go into the wheat,

And blow there on my hartshorn, so
That all my friends can hear thee blow."

"Al in het koren en gaen ik niet,
Op uwen horen en blaes ik niet!"

"Gaet ginder onder de galge
En haelt daer een pot met zalve
En strykt dat aen myn rooden hals!"

"Al onder de galge en gaen ik niet
Uw rooden hals en stryk ik niet:
Moordenaers raed en doe ik niet!"

Zy nam het hoofd al by het haer
En waschtet in een bronne klaer.

Zy zette haer schrylings op het ros:
Al zingend en klingend reed zy doort bosch.

En als zy was ter halver baen,
Kwam Halewyns moeder daer gegaen:
"Schoon maegt, zaegt gy myn zoon niet gaen?"

"Uw zoon heer Halewyn is gaen jagen:
G'en ziet hem weer uws levens dagen!

Uw zoon heer Halewyn is dood
Ik heb zyn hoofd in mynen schoot:
Van bloed is myn voorschoot rood!"

Toen ze aen haers vaders poorte kwam,
Zy blaesde den horen als een man.

En als de vader dit vernam,
't Verheugde hem dat zy weder kwam.

Daer wierd gehouden een banket,
Het hoofd werd op de tafel gezet.

"Among the wheat I will not go,
Upon thine horn I will not blow."

"Go yonder under the gallows' beam.
Get me a jar of anointing cream."

"I go not under the gallows' joint.
Thy blood-red neck I won't anoint."

She lifted the head by its long hair,
And washed it in a fountain clear.

She mounted astride upon the steed,
And singing and ringing rode through the glade.

When she was gone halfway the wood,
She came where Halewin's mother stood.

"Beautiful maiden, tell me, pray,
Hast seen my son along the way?"

"Sir Halewin is a-hunting gone.
Thou never wilt see again thy son.

Thy son, Sir Halewin, is dead.
Here in my lap I carry his head."

She came to her father's gate at last.
She blew the horn with a manlike blast.

Her father heard her blow the horn.
Glad he was to see her return.

They made a feast of one accord.
The head was placed upon the board.

tr. Adriaan Barnouw

[HET DAGHET INDEN OOSTEN]
Een oudt liedeken

"Het daghet inden oosten,
Het lichtet overal.
Hoe luttel weet mijn liefken,
Och, waer ick henen sal."

"Och warent al mijn vrienden
dat mijn vianden zijn!
Ick voerde u uuten lande,
Mijn lief, mijn minnekijn."

"Dats waer soudi mi voeren,
Stout ridder wel gemeyt?
ic ligge in mijns liefs armkens
Met grooter waerdicheyt."

"Ligdy in uus liefs armen?
Bilo, ghi en segt niet waer!
Gaet henen ter linde groene,
Versleghen zo leyt hi daer."

Tmeysken nam haren mantel
Ende si ghinc eenen ganck
Al totter linde groene,
daer si den dooden vant.

"Och, ligdy hier verslaghen,
Versmoort al in u bloet?
dat heeft gedaen u roemen
Ende uwen hooghen moet.

Och, lichdy hier verslaghen,
die mi te troosten plach?
Wath hebdy mi ghelaten?
So menighen droeven dach."

Tmeysken nam haren mantel
Ende si ghinck eenen ganck
Al voor haers vaders poorte,
die si ontsloten vant.

[THE EAST'S ALIGHT WITH DAWNING]
An Old Song*

"The East's alight with dawning,
New day hath spread its glow.
How little knows my lover—
Alas, where can I go?"

"If all who bear me hatred
Were suddenly my friends,
I'd flee with thee, my dearest,
Beyond where this land ends."

"Is that, knight brave and gallant,
Where thou wouldst carry me?
I lie in my lief's arms, though,
With greater dignity."

"In thy lief's arms, thou sayest?
By Jove, that's not the truth!
Look under the green linden,
He lies there dead, thy youth."

The maiden took her mantle
And went her troubled way
In haste to the green linden,
And found her lover slain.

"Oh, dost thou lie here lifeless,
Blood flowing from thy side?
This comes of thy rash boasting
And overweening pride.

Oh, dost thou lie here lifeless,
Who brought me such good cheer?
What hast thou left me now, love?
Sad days are all, I fear."

The maiden took her mantle
And went her troubled way
In haste unto her father
And found his gate unchained.

---

* This traditional ballad is structured as a dialogue between a young woman, who has waited all night long in vain for her lover, and another suitor who, appearing outside her window, announces that he would like to abduct her to his country. The young woman proudly refuses.[1]

"Och, is hier eenich heere
Oft eenich edel man,
die mi mijnen dooden
Begraven helpen can?"

Die heeren sweghen stille,
Si en maecten gheen geluyt.
dat meysken keerde haer omme,
Si ghinc al weenende uut.

Si nam hem in haren armen,
Si custe hem voor den mont
In eender corter wijlen
Tot also menigher stont.

Met sinen blancken swaerde
dat si die aerde op groef;
Met haer snee witten armen
Ten grave dat si hem droech.

"Nu wil ic mi gaen begeven
In een cleyn cloosterkijn
Ende draghen swarte wijlen
Ende worden een nonnekijn."

Met haer claer stemme
Die misse dat si sanck,
Met haer snee witten handen
Dat si dat belleken clanck.

[DEN DAGH EN WIL NIET VERBORGHEN ZIJN]

"Den dach en wil niet verborghen zijn,
Het is schoon dach, dat duncket mi.
Mer wie verborghen heeft zijn lief,
Hoe noode ist dat si scheyden."

"Wachter, nu laet u schimpen zijn
Ende laet hi slapen, die alder liefste mijn.
een vingerlinck root sal ic u schincken,
Wildy den dach niet melden."

"Och meldic hem niet, rampsalich wijf,
Het gaet den jongelinck aen zijn lijf."
"Hebdy den schilt, ick hebbe die speyr,
daer mede maect u van heyr."

"Oh, is there any knight here
Or any noble man
Who'll bury my poor loved one?
Do help me if you can."

The knights sat there in silence,
They uttered not a word.
The maiden rose to leave them,
Weeping as she turned.

She took him in her arms then,
And placed her mouth on his,
And filled a few short moments
With kiss on tender kiss.

His shining sword she wielded
To dig the turf away;
Her snow-white hands toiled bravely
Till in his grave he lay.

"Now I will go and find me
A little nunnery.
All black will be my clothing,
My gems a rosary."

Her sweet voice echoed clearly
In every mass they sang,
And little bells for prayers
With snow-white hands she rang.

tr. Myra Scholz

[THE DAY WILL NO MORE HIDDEN BE]

"The day will no more hidden be,
the day has come, it seems to me.
But those who've hidden a sweetheart
How loath they are to part."

"Watchman, leave off your odious words
And let him sleep, my dearest love.
I'll give you a ring of pure red gold
If you don't call out the day."

"If I don't call it, unhappy maid,
The young man with his life will pay."
"You have the shield, I have the spear,
So get you now away from here."

Die jonghelinck sliep ende hi ontspranck,
Die liefste hi in zijn armen nam:
"En latet u niet so na ter herten gaen,
Ick come noch tavont weder."

Die jonghelinck op zijn vale ros tradt,
Die vrouwe op hooger tinnen lach.
Si sach so verre noortwaert inne
Den dach door die wolcken op dringhen.

"Had ick den slotel vanden daghe,
Ic weerpen in gheender wilden Masen,
Oft vander Masen tot inden Rijn,
Al en soude hi nemmeer vonden zijn."

[DIE NACHTEGAEL DIE SANCK EEN LIEDT]

"Die nachtegael die sanck een liedt, dat leerde ick,
ick hebber een verholen lief, die vrijde ick;
en die wil ick niet laeten, iae laten;
ick hope noch een cort half nacht
in myns liefs arms te slapen."

Die moeder van den bedde spranc, ontstac haer licht;
sy vant haer jongste dochter op haer bedde nicht:
"waer is sy nu ghegangen, ia gangen?
Nu is myn jongste dochter weech
met een soo vreemde manne."

"Hy en was my alsoo vreemde niet, hy had my lief;
hy voerde my al over die hey, hy misdede my niet.
Hy voerde my over die heyden, iae heyden;
daer twee schoon liefkens t'samen gaen,
hoe noode ist dat sy scheyden.

Daer twee goe liefkens t'samen aen den danse gaen,
hoe vriendelic dat sy haer oochskens op malcander slaen,
ghelyck die morghen sterre, iae sterre;
myn herteken is van sulcker aert:
bruyn oochskens sie ick gaeren.

The young man slept and then awoke
And took his loved one in his arms:
"Don't take it so to heart, my love,
I will come back tonight."

The young man mounted his pale horse,
The lady stood on the ramparts high.
Far and away in the North she saw
The daylight pierce the clouds.

"If I were to have the key of the day,
Into the river I'd throw it away
Or from the Meuse up to the Rhine
Though it would never be found again."

tr. Anneke Prins

[THE NIGHTINGALE SANG A SONG]

"The nightingale sang a song, I learned it,
I have a secret love, I loved him;
I do not want to leave him, leave him;
Let me yet sleep one short half night
In my lover's arms."

The mother awoke and the candle she lit;
Her youngest daughter she found not in bed.
"Now where has she gone, oh gone?
My youngest daughter, she's gone away,
With a stranger she has gone."

"No stranger to me, he loved me well;
He took me away, and he treated me well.
He took me over the heath, the heath;
When two young lovers together lie
How loath they are to part.

Where two young lovers a-dancing go,
How sweetly they look at each other so
Just like the morning star, the star;
This is my selfsame nature too:
Brown eyes do warm my heart.

Myn harteken is veel wilder dan een wilt conyn;
dat en mach niemant temmen dan die liefste mijn;
dat en mach niemant temmen, jae temmen,
en waer die alderliefste myn;
dat is so fraeyen gheselle.
Och waren alle duivels so,
en ick voer inder helle!"

DE PLOEGTREKKER

luistert oud en jonk van jaren
die nog leeft in dezen tijd
'tgeen ik u zal openbaren
van een grote misdadigheid
het klonk ons in de oren
toen wij het kwamen te horen
dat er 'ne man moest voor de ploeg
't was beter dan in de kroeg

opeens had hij zijne vrouw geslagen
en de geburen dan ook niet min
staken de koppen al bij elkaren
loerden dan op diejen bozen vent
ze zagen met verlangen
en zochten hem te vangen
ze riepen met een groot geluid
ruk hem de deur maar uit

denkt eens hoe hij stond verslagen
toen de vrouwen kwamen af
men heeft zijn vonnis voorgelezen
en ze geven hem zijn straf
gij zult hier niet aan mankeren
wij zullen 't u wel afleren
dat gij uw vrouw ooit nog zult slaan
voor de ploeg zult gij trekken gaan

denk eens hoe hij stond te beven
en hoe hij al stond in het zweet
toen er die vrouwen bezig gingen
maakten het tuig van het paard gereed
het zijn bij al geen gekken
die hem voor de ploeg doen trekken
met ene zweep al in de hand
zo duwen ze hem naar het land

My heart is wilder than the rabbit in the field;
no other may tame it than my sweetheart;
no one may tame it, yes tame it
None other than my dearest.
So lively and free, I love him well.
Oh, if all devils were like that,
I would go down to Hell!"

tr. Anneke Prins

THE SONG OF THE PLOW [2]

Listen old and young in years
All still living at this time
And I will now reveal to you
The story of a grievous crime
This is the tale as it appears
Though we could hardly believe our ears:
A man who'd rather drink and bet
Was forced to pull the plow instead

He beat his wife one fateful day
So the neighbors all came out
And together they planned a way
To take revenge on that rotten lout
All distressed and all distraught
They were determined to have him caught
And they shouted loud and clear
Get that bully out of here

Just imagine how he trembled
When the women were assembled
For his final sentencing
And their punishment was grim:
We will teach you to refrain
From ever beating your wife again
You will pay us what you owe
You are sentenced to pull the plow

Just imagine how he trembled
And how the sweat began to pour
When the womenfolk assembled
On his back the horse's gear
Surely they were not fools
Who made him pull and pull and pull
Cracking whips held in their hands
They chased him onto the land

op het land al aangekomen
riep hij het is het paard zijne stiel
vrouwtjes wilt mij toch vergeven
hij trok dat hij ter aarde viel
ik zal van heel mijn leven
mijn vrouw geen klap meer geven
'k zal doen gelijk enen braven man
van de ploeg ben ik zo bang

nu ga ik mijn sluiten geven
't is een les voor jan en piet
wilt er uwe vrouw geen klappen geven
want de ploeg die staat gereed
er is geen beter lere
maar ik deed 't ook niet gere
ik zit liever in de kroeg
als te trekken voor de ploeg

ANNE MARIEKEN

Wel Anne Marieken, waer gaet gy naer toe?
Wel Anne Marieken, waer gaet gy naer toe?
"'k Gane naer buiten al by de soldaten,"
Hoepsasa, falhala, Anne Marie.

Wel Anne Marieken, wat gaet gy daer doen?
Wel Anne Marieken, wat gaet gy daer doen?
"Haspen en spinnen, soldaetjes beminnen,"
Hoepsasa, falhala, Anne Marie.

Wel Anne Marieken, hebt gy er geen man?
Wel Anne Marieken, hebt gy er geen man?
"Heb ik geen man ik kryge geen slagen,"
Hoepsasa, falhala, Anne Marie.

When he faced the plowing field
He cried, women have mercy please
This plow only horses should wield
And he pulled until he fell to his knees:
Never again in all my life
Will I lash out at my dear wife
I'll behave like a humble man
To avoid the plough, if indeed I can

And here my story comes to an end
It is a lesson for every man
If you beat your wife, if ever you do
The plow will be waiting here for you
There is in the world no better cure
And I myself would avoid it for sure
In pubs I'd rather drink and bet
Than be forced to pull the plow instead

tr. J. H. and J. W. Prins

ANNE MARIEKEN*

"Say Anne Marieken, where do you go?
Say Anne Marieken, where do you go?"
"I'm going outside to look at the soldiers,"
Hopsasa faldera, Anne Marie.†

"Say Anne Marieken, then what will you do?
Say Anne Marieken, then what will you do?"
"Carding and spinning and kissing the soldiers,"
Hopsasa faldera, Anne Marie.

"Say Anne Marieken, then have you no man?
Say Anne Marieken, then have you no man?"
"Don't have a man, won't get any beatings,"
Hopsasa faldera, Anne Marie.

* The translator changed the position of the quotation marks, which the editor
(J. F. Willems) arbitrarily put into the orally transmitted Dutch text in 1848. It seems
more logical that the question with which every stanza opens is answered by the lusty
Anne Marieke in the third line of every stanza.

† "Hopsasa faldera" are words without specific meaning apart from their sound value.
They are used to suggest a frivolous dance rhythm comparable to "tra la la."

Wel Anne Marieken, hebt gy er geen kind?
Wel Anne Marieken, hebt gy er geen kind?
"Heb ik geen kind, 'k moete niet zorgen;"
Hoepsasa, falhala, Anne Marie.

LIED V

Al droevet die tijt ende die vogheline,
Dan darf niet doen die herte fine
Die dore minne wilt doghen pine.
    Hi sal weten ende kinnen al
    —Suete ende wreet,
    Lief ende leet—
    Wat men ter minnen pleghen sal.

Die fiere, die daer toe sijn ghedeghen
Dat si onghecuster minnen pleghen,
Si selen in allen weghen daer jeghen
    Stout sijn ende coene,
    Ende al ghereet te ontfaen
    Si troest, si slaen,
    Van minnen doene.

Der minnen pleghen es onghehoert,
Als hi wel kint dies hevet becoert,
Want si in midden den troest testoert.
    Hine can ghedueren
    Dien minne gheraect;
    hi ghesmaect
    Vele onghenoemder uren.

"Say Anne Marieken, and have you no child?
Say Anne Marieken, and have you no child?"
"Don't have a child, so I don't have a worry,"
Hopsasa faldera, Anne Marie.

tr. Anneke Prins

HADEWIJCH (13TH CENTURY)

SONG V*

Though sad the season and the birds
The noble heart need never break
That suffers pain for Love's dear sake.
    Well it knows what must be faced—
    Bitter and sweet,
    Joys and griefs—
    By those enamored of Love's ways.

The valiant ones who have come so far
That unfulfilled Love is all they desire
Down every road pursue their quest,
    Intrepid and bold,
    Ready for all,
    Be it solace or blows,
    That Love bestows.

The ways of Love defy all telling,
As he well knows who has been enthralled,
For midway in bliss She withdraws it all.
    One touched by Love's power
    Can hardly endure
    The taste of so many
    Unspeakable hours.[†]

---

* Hadewijch's theology assumes that we have a twofold life: on earth in our created self, and with God in our ideal self. This leads to an untiring, intense striving to identify our created self with the self that is in God. A merging with our eternal, original image can be attained through the force of Love, *Minne.* Thus Minne, often personified or conceptualized in distinctly unfeminine and passionate terms, is the central figure of the poems. Minne is inexhaustible: every *ghenoechte* (satisfaction) leads to more *begherte* (desire), in an endless dialectic.

[†] The series of antitheses referring to Love, which begin each of the four remaining stanzas of the poem, will develop what is meant by these "hours."

Bi wilen heet, bi wilen cout,
Bi wilen bloede, bi wilen bout:
Hare onghedueren es menichfout.
  Die minne al maent
  Die grote scout
  Haerre riker ghewout
  Daer si ons toe spaent.

Bi wilen lief, bi wilen leet.
Bi wilen verre, bi wilen ghereet:
Die dit met trouwen van minnen versteet,
  Dat es jubileren:
  Hoe minne versleet
  Ende omme veet
  In een hanteren.

Bi wilen ghenedert, bi wilen ghehoghet,
Bi wilen verborghen, bi wilen vertoghet.
Eer selc van minnen wert ghesoghet
  Doghet hi grote avontuere,
  Eer hi gheraect
  Daer hi ghesmaect
  Der minnen natuere.

Bi wilen licht, bi wilen swaer,
Bi wilen doncker, bi wilen claer,
In vrien troest, in bedwonghenne vaer,
  In nemen ende in gheven,
  Moeten die sinne
  Die dolen in minne,
  Altoes hier leven.

NEGENDE BRIEF

God doe u weten, lieve kint, wie hi es ende wies hi pleghet met sinen knecht-
en, ende nameleke met sinen meiskenen; ende verslende u in hem. Daer
de diepheit siere vroetheit es, daer sal hi u leren wat hi es, ende hoe won-
derleke soeteleke dat een lief in dat ander woent, ende soe dore dat ander
woent, dat haerre en gheen hem selven en onderkent. Mer si ghebruken
onderlinghe ende elc anderen, mont in mont, ende herte in herte, ende
lichame in lichame, ende ziele in ziele, ende ene soete godlike nature doer
hen beiden vloyende, ende si beide een dore hen selven, ende al eens beide
bliven, ja ende blivende.

Sometimes hot, at other times cold,
Now so timid, then overbold—
Inconstant She is in so many ways.
    Love serves summons
    For the large debt owed
    To Her sovereign might
    That lures us and holds.

At times full of spite, at other times kind,
Now far away, then close at our side—
To understand this about Love's ploys
    Is to truly rejoice:
    How a blow from above
    And an ardent embrace
    Are one act of Love.

At times raised high, at others laid low,
Now hidden away, then open to view,
The full breast of Love is only for those
    Who risks great adventure
    En route to the place
    Where at last they may taste
    Of Love's true nature.

Sometimes heavy, sometimes light,
Now all darkness, then clear and bright;
In freedom comfort, in narrow straits fear,
    In taking and giving
    They must ever be living,
    Those brave hearts errant,
    Roving in Love.

        tr. Myra Scholz

NINTH LETTER

May God make known to you, dear child, who he is, and how intimately
he deals with his servants, particularly with his handmaidens. May he swal-
low you up into himself. There, in the abyss of his wisdom, he will teach
you what he is and how wondrously sweet it is for one lover to dwell in
the other, and for them so to permeate each other that neither can dis-
tinguish himself from the other. But they taste the fruit of love together,
giving and receiving, mouth in mouth, heart in heart, body in body, and
soul in soul, with one sweet divine nature flowing through both of them,
the two selves having merged into one while at the same time remaining
two—and, indeed, so they remain forever.

        tr. Myra Scholz

DE PARADOXEN DER LIEFDE

Dat suetste van minnen sijn hare storme;
Haer diepste afgront es haer scoenste vorme;
In haer verdolen dats na gheraken;
Om haer verhongeren dats voeden ende smaken;
Hare mestroest es seker wesen;
Hare seerste wonden es al ghenesen;
Om hare verdoyen dat es gheduren;
Hare berghen es vinden alle vren;
Om hare quelen dat es ghesonde;
Hare helen openbaert hare conde;
Hare onthouden sijn hare ghichten;
Sonder redenne es hare scoenste dichten;
Hare gheuangnesse es al verloest;
Hare seerste slaen es hare suetste troest;
Hare al berouen es groot vromen;
Hare henen varen es naerre comen;
Hare nederste stille es hare hoechste sanc;
Hare groetste abolghe es hare liefste danc;
Hare groetste dreighen es al trouwe;
Hare droefheit es boete van allen rouwe;
Hare rijcheit es hare al ghebreken.
Noch machmen meer van minnen spreken:
Hare hoechste trouwe doet neder sinken;
Hare hoechste wesen doet diep verdrincken;
Hare grote rijcheit maect armoede;
Haers vele vercreghen toent onspoede;
Hare troesten maect die wonden groot;
Hare hanteren brinct meneghe doet;
Hare voeden es hongher; hare kinnen es dolen;
Verleidinghe es wijse van harer scolen;
Hare hanteren sijn storme wreet;
Hare ghedueren es in onghereet;
Hare toenen es hare seluen al helen;
Hare ghichten sijn mere weder stelen;
Hare gheloeften sijn al verleiden;
Hare chierheiden sijn al oncleiden;
Hare waerheit es al bedrieghen;
Hare sekerheyt scijnt meneghen lieghen,

THE PARADOXES OF LOVE

What is sweetest in Love is her tempestuousness;
Her deepest abyss is her most beautiful form;
To lose one's way in her is to touch her close at hand;
To die of hunger for her is to feed and taste;
Her despair is assurance;
Her sorest wounding is all curing;*
To waste away for her sake is to be in repose;
Her hiding is finding at all hours;
To languish for her sake is to be in good health;
Her concealment reveals what can be known of her;
Her retentions are her gifts;
Wordlessness is her most beautiful utterance;
Imprisonment by her is total release;
Her sorest blow is her sweetest consolation;
Her ruthless robbery is great profit;
Her withdrawal is approach;
Her deepest silence is her sublime song;
Her greatest wrath is her dearest thanks;
Her greatest threat is pure fidelity;
Her sadness is the alleviation of all pain.
We can say yet more about Love:
Her wealth is her lack of everything;
Her truest fidelity brings about our fall;
Her highest being drowns us in the depths;
Her great wealth bestows pauperism;
Her largesse proves to be our bankruptcy;
Her tender care enlarges our wounds;
Association with her brings death over and over;
Her table is hunger; her knowledge is error;
Seduction is the custom of her school;
Encounters with her are cruel storms;
Rest in her is in the unreachable;
Her revelation is the total hiding of herself;
Her gifts, besides, are thieveries;
Her promises are all seductions;
Her adornments are all undressing;
Her truth is all deception;
To many her assurance appears to lie—

* Job 5:18.

Dies ic ende menich dat orconde
Wel moghen draghen in alre stonde,
Dien de minnen dicken heuet ghetoent
Saken daer wij bi sijn ghehoent,
Ende waenden hebben dat hare bleef.
Sint si mi ierst die treken dreef
Ende ic ghemercte al hare seden,
So hildicker mi al anders mede:
Hare ghedreich, hare ghelouen,
Daer met en werdic meer bedroghen.
Ic wille hare wesen al datse si,
Si goet, si fel: al eens eest mi.

REFEREYN XXVII
Gemaect int jaer vijfthien hondert twintich en vijve,
Januarij twalef, jonstich van bedrijve

a.
Ghij proper meyskens, ghij enghe dierkens,
En jonge gesellen, wildt van manierkens,
Wildt u niet zo schierkens om houwen stellen.
Ghij speelt nu bij nachte lustich en fierkens
Voor uus liefs duerken met herpen, met lierkens.
Zij troten als mierkens, dees jonge gesellen,
Om houwen sij vrienden en magen quellen.
En wilt u niet versnellen, sijt coel van sinne;
Die vruchten des houwelijcx wil ic vertellen.
Willet wel spellen, wat houwen heeft inne:
Al schijnt de liefde zeer heet ten beginne,
Sorge doet de minne slappen alle dage,
Sij maeckt cousen vol palingen, een scerpe kinne
En caken dinne; hoort wat ic gewage:
Het waer goet houwen, maer tsorgen es de plage.

b.
Alsoo saen als de brulocht es gheëndt,
Zoo beghindt de sorghe, waer ghij u keerdt oft wendt;
Om largent men sendt van allen sijen.
Esser tgheldt dan dinne, zoo eest hof geschendt.
Waer blijft dan darm brugom? Jongers, dit bekendt,

This is the witness that can be truly borne
At any moment by me and many others
To whom Love has often shown
Wonders by which we were mocked,
Imagining we possessed what she kept back for herself.
After she first played these tricks on me,
And I considered all her methods,
I went to work in a wholly different way:
By her threats and her promises
I was no longer deceived.
I will belong to her, whatever she may be,
Gracious or merciless; to me it is all one!

tr. Mother Columba Hart

ANNA BIJNS (1493–ca. 1575)

REFRAIN XXVII
Made in January, on the twelfth day,
in fifteen twenty-five anno domine.

a.
You well-bred girls, you timid things,
And lads with your shenanigans,
Don't be in such a rush to marry.
At night with harps and lyres you hurry
To our doors singing bold and merry song.
These fellows come in droves, like ants.
Family and friends they nag: oh, for a chance
To marry! Calm down, keep cool, don't rush headlong.
Since you should know the fruits you'll reap
I'll tell you what it means to marry.
Though love at first seems ardent, worry
Makes flames flicker where they used to leap.
Care puts runs in stockings, a point on a chin,
Gauntness in cheeks. Can you take all this in?
Marriage would be fine if it weren't plagued with worry.

b.
No sooner is the wedding past
Than cares crowd in on every side.
Your pocketbook will shrivel fast,
And once your money's gone, so is your pride.
Then what's the poor bridegroom to do?

Als ghij loopt en rendt om houwen, om vrijen:
Dan moettij gaen slaven, seldij bedijen,
En vruecht vertijen, hoort vrouwen en mannen.
Sober gewin doet ooc zelden verblijen;
Dan esser al lijen, vruecht esser gebannen,
Daer ghebreken schotelen, potten en cannen,
Teylen en pannen, tafele en scrage;
Cundij niet gewinnen, zoo heet ghij een hannen.
Die dus es gespannen, sie dat hijt verdrage.
Het waer goet houwen, maer tsorgen es de plage.

c.

Dan werdt hij Jan splijtmijte; eens verquiste hij tgoedt,
Nu telt hij de gortte; eerst had hij eenen moedt,
Dees arm bloedt nu alle solaes ontbeerdt.
Die voortijds zoo milde was, es nu soo vroedt;
Wat hij werckt oft slaeft, tes al tegenspoedt.
Hij dunckt mij verwoedt, die een wijf begeerdt;
Tes een plage boven plage, bij Gans peerdt.
Eenen couden heerdt, turf noch hout om branden,
Peyst hier om, jongers, hier voor sijt verveerdt.
Dan werden verteerdt juwelen en panden.
Het es quaet neringe doen met ijdelen handen,
En geen broodt in de tanden maeckt een ijdel mage.
Elck wacht hem te springen in zelcken banden,
Opdat hij met schanden na niet en clage:
Het waer goet houwen, maer tsorgen es de plage.

d.

Dan esser Beele: aeylaschen, wachermen,
Wat dede ic gehoudt, Godt moets ontfermen!
Dan sijn de termen kijven en vloeken,
De fradden ooc aen de ooren zwermen.
Deen crijt van couwen, dander van honger kermen;
Dan moet Jan ooc wermen der kinder doeken.
Tes: vader geeft appelen, moeder geeft koeken,
Men dichter af boeken, zij wetent diet gevoelen;
Het esser hooftzweer in allen hoeken.
Dan eest: wildt gelt soeken om wiegen, om stoelen;
Deene wilt eeten, dander kacken oft poelen.
Noeyt zelcken woelen, tverleede hem diet saghe.
Eest kindt dan bedreten, soo moeten sijt spoelen;
Dit doet liefde coelen, die groot was van behage.
Het waer goet houwen, maer tsorgen es de plage.

Remember this, lads, in your rush to get married:
You'll work like a slave, be weary and harried,
And find little joy in it all. Men, women too,
Listen to me. Hard-earned money doesn't go
Very far. Just think of the problems you'll face.
You'll need pots and pans then, pitchers and plates,
Tubs, tables and chairs. You'll earn what you can,
But if that's not enough they'll say you're not really a man.
Along with this yoke comes a great load to carry.
Marriage would be fine if it weren't plagued with worry.

c.
Penny-pinching Peter is what he becomes.
He used to spend freely, now he counts all his crumbs.
Once he had courage, in trouble he's spineless;
His hand is now closed that was open in kindness.
However hard he may toil or slave,
Fortune keeps frowning. It's crazy to crave
For a wife, I say, like wishing for floods and the plague.
A hearth that's gone cold, no peat and no wood,
Just think of it, fellows. Feel frightened? You should!
Your jewels and other fine things you will pawn,
But when they're used up and your bread is all gone
Your stomach will simply go rumbling on.
This snare you'll fall into when bagging your quarry.
Beware—or we'll hear you shamefacedly moan:
Marriage would be fine if it weren't plagued with worry.

d.
Then Nelly starts up: Alas, woe is me!
Why did I marry? God pity me!
And all the talk turns to scolding and cursing
While swarms of children buzz at your ears.
One cries, "I'm cold!", the other wants nursing.
Where's Peter? Drying diapers for all the little dears.
It's cookies from mother, apples from father—
Books make it sound sweet, they don't mention the bother.
Wherever you look there are headaches and cares,
Such as where to find money for cradles and chairs.
Now this one is hungry, that one has to pee;
The chaos is total—and painful to see.
Each filthy bottom has to be cleaned.
All this makes passion cool off in a hurry.
Marriage would be fine if it weren't plagued with worry.

e.

Princen, princessen, die treden Venus paden,
Blijft ongebonden, ic sout u raden,
Wilt dit pack niet laden, wacht u voor den stoot,
Loopt niet zeere om houwen, maer gaet met staden;
Peyst, hongerighe buycken sijn quaet om versaden
Metter scappraden, daermen broodt buyten sloot.
Veel kinder breeken thoodt, geen sorge soo groot;
Eene opten schoot, noch eene int lijf,
Drije, viere omden heerdt, zij maecken u bloot;
Al haddij scepen, boot, gij werdt een catijf,
God zoude vereezelen, troude hij een wijf.
Meyskens, houdt u oock stijf, sijt om houwen trage;
Al dunckt u nu tvrijen goet tijdtverdrijf,
Twerdt na wel gekijf; diet proeven ic vrage.
Het waer goet houwen, maer tsorgen es de plage.

AEN JUFFROUWE ANNA MARIA SCHUERMANS

Sijt gegroet, ô Jonge Bloem,
Van wiens kennis dat ik roem,
Die ik acht en' die ik minne,
Die ik hou voor mijn vriendinne:
Die in toecomende tijdt
(Immers soo 't den Hemel lijdt)
'T puijk sal wesen van die maechden,
Die ooijt wetenschap bejaechden.
Lieffelijke, soete spruijt,
Schiet vrij deuchdes looten uijt:
En' de schoonheidt van uw' leden,
Ciert die met noch schoonder zeden.
Laet uw' lieve, kleene mondt,
Als het past, met reen en' grondt,
Mannen hoochmoedt doen verdwijnen;

e.

Princes, princesses, who walk the paths of Venus,
Take my advice, don't tie any knots. What I mean is:
Don't take on this burden as if you were blind.
Don't rush into marriage, go slow, take your time.
Remember that poor hungry mouths can't be filled
When cupboards are empty and the breadbox has nil.
No worry is greater than too many offspring,
One on your lap, one more in the offing
And round the hearth three or four—they'll strip you bare,
Though ships you may own and fine silverware.
If God were to marry he'd be a jackass.
You girls, hold back, too. You may think that to pass
Your time wooing is pleasant. Why don't you ask
Those who've learned? Later it's all hurly-burly.
Marriage would be fine if it weren't plagued with worry.

tr. Myra Scholz

ANNA ROEMERS VISSCHER (1584–1651)

TO MISS ANNA MARIA SCHUERMANS*

Hail! O bright young flower, hail!
Whose wisdom I do sing the praise,
Whom I respect and I do love,
Whom I do hold to be my friend,
Who is to be the future queen
(Should Heaven be so willing)
Of all fair maidens in the world,
Who Science ever have pursued.
O sweet and kindly bud
Freely shoots of virtue sprout,
And let the beauty of your limbs
Adornèd be with moral grace.
Let your sweet small mouth,
When opportune, banish male pride
With reason and with argument,

---

* Anna Roemers addresses her contemporary, Anna Maria van Schurman (1607–1678) who—as an exceptionally learned woman—was to become a celebrity. In this poem Anna Roemers is possibly aiming at installing a role model for other talented young women and encouraging liberal fathers to educate their daughters just as thoroughly.

Als gij Grieken en' latijnen,
Dat geleerd' uijtheemsche volk,
Toe kent spreken, zonder tolk.
Dat uw' witt' en' teeder handen
Al de schrijvers maek tot schanden.
Als gij lijnwaet, met uw naeldt;
Of papier, met kool, bemaelt:
Dat de konstenaers staen kijken,
En' bij Pallas u gelijken.
Als gij met de vingers dan
Roert de Clavecimbel an,
Of de luijt; en' daer het zingen
Aerdich onder weet te mingen.
Aeij! hoe geestich moet dat gaen?
Hoe bevallich moet dat staen?
'K wensch dat godt uw 's levens jaren
Wil voor ongeval bewaren.
Eer uw' Vader hebben moet,
Die u wel heeft op-gevoedt.

AEN JUFFROUW JOHANNA COMANS
Daer ten Eeten sijnde op een Roemer Gheschreven

Kond ick Sonder wee of smart
U doen kijken jn myn hert,
Ghij soudt meer als ghij verwacht,
Siên hoe veel dat ic u Acht,
Daer ick t'alderminste van
Op dit glas Niet Schrijven Can.

When to Romans and to Greeks,
That learnèd alien folk,
You speak directly in their tongue.
May your white and tender hands
Put writers all to shame.
When you work linen with your needle,
Or paper with charcoalèd lines,
May artists come to stand and watch
And you with Pallas then compare.
When lightly with your fingertips
You touch the harpsichord or lute,
You then know how to mingle well
Singing in among their strains.
Ah! How airy that will sound!
How graceful will that be to see!
I wish that God the watch will keep
'Gainst mishap throughout all your years,
Let honor to your Father come
Who educated you so well.

tr. Tony Briggs

TO MISS JOHANNA COMANS*
Inscribed on a wine glass when dining at her home

But for the pain and sore distress
My heart would open to your view
And show much more than you can guess
Of honor and respect for you—
The least of it would far surpass
What I can write upon this glass.

tr. Myra Scholz

* Johanna Comans was a friend and poet from Middelburg. Anna engraved this poem
with a diamond needle on a goblet while dining at her home.

AEN JOFFVROUW GEORGETTE DE MONTENEIJ

Georgette, Eij vergeeft het mij
Dat ick soo stout vermetel sij
Dat ick in onse duytsche tael
Van woort tot woort niet altemael
'T francoys ghevolght heb, noch u sin
Recht wt gebeelt: maar smeet daar in
't goetduncken van mijn cleyn verstant.
Doe ick u boeck creech inde hant
'T heeft mij soo wonder-wel behaacht,
te meer omdat het van een Maacht
Gheschreven was. Dat docht my gróót.
Ick wenschte Sulcken speelgenóót
Maer cant int Lichaem niet gheschiên,
Mijn Geest zal Lijckwel bij u vliên.

MUYTERIJ TEGEN CUPIDO

Al ben ick nu gequetst, ô wicht! soo sal ick maecken
Dat ick, naer u begeer, niet quijnen sal of craecken,
 Ghy sult u wensch niet sien, dat ick als mal en sot
 Nu sou begaen daer ick soo vaack mé heb ghespot,
Dat ick door schrick van pijn klijn-seerich sou verschuylen
Mijn wonden, op dat die verettren en vervuylen.
 Siet daer mé gae ick heen, en soeck sulck een die can
 (Ervaren in die const) mijn vrylick tasten an;
Ick sal gheen bijt-salf noch gheen pijnlick tenten vreesen,
Noch bittre drancken die bequaem zijn te gheneesen
 Mijn hert van dese quael, die 'k in mijn jonge tijt
 Soo angstich heb gevreest, zoo naerstich heb gemijt,

TO MISS GEORGETTE DE MONTENEIJ*

Georgette, kindly pardon me,
I've been so bold, perhaps too free
When rendering your poetry
Into my native Dutch. You'll see
I didn't always find a way
To shape the meanings you convey
But humbly used my own good sense.
Your book afforded me immense
Delight right from the first.
What's more, this was a maiden's verse!
That I admired—wished dearly, too,
For a playmate such as you.
Though in the body this can't be,
Our spirits know no boundary.

                tr. Myra Scholz

REVOLT AGAINST CUPID †

Though I am wounded, little imp, I will not pine
Away as you would like, nor mope nor moan nor whine.
You'll never have your way and see me play the fool
At all the silly games I've always ridiculed.
My wounds I will not hide for fear of facing pain,
For they'll start festering and dangerously inflame.
I'll simply find someone experienced in the art
Of treating injuries like mine. The salve may smart,
I'm not afraid; the probing knife I'll not refuse;
And, bitter though they be, I'll drink the healing brews
To cure this ailment of the heart, that I so feared
And mightily resisted through all my younger years.

* Georgette de Monteneij was a French poet, whose Cent Emblêmes Chrestiens Anna translated into Dutch.

† This poem addresses several deities from ancient Greek mythology. First the lyrical "I" speaks to Cupid ("little imp"). Next she addresses Pallas Athena (the "helmeted Maiden," virgin goddess of learning and wisdom). She cannot bear to hear Cupid praise the beauty of his mother (Aphrodite, goddess of love) and denigrate that of Athena. This is an allusion to the famous mythological beauty contest in which the Trojan shepherd Paris had to give a golden apple to the fairest of three goddesses: Athena, Aphrodite, or Hera. Paris chose Aphrodite, since she promised to let the beautiful Helen fall in love with him. In the last line the poet refers to the catastrophic Trojan war, waged for the possession of Helen.

En ghy gehelmde Maecht, ghy schoonste der Goddinnen,
Hoe mocht het van u hert dat ghy my liet verwinnen?
    Hoe mocht het van u hert, dat die u altijt eert
    Soo klackloos van een kint! een kint! nu is verneert?
Ick berst van spijt, als my dees aeterlingsche-bastert
Sijns moeders schoonheyt prijst, en uwe schoonheyt lastert.
    Neen, neen, ick acht soo veel geen lichaem schoon en fris,
    Als een oprecht gemoet daer deucht gewortelt is,
Al creech sijn moer de prijs, nae 't oordeel van een Herder
Die op sijn geyle lust slech sach en niet eens verder,
    Dat acht ick niet met al: wanneer men siet het endt
    Wat was zijn loon? ach arm! slech jammer en ellendt
Wie souw niet uyt sijn hert de dertel min-lust royen
Die de puyn-berghen siet van het verbrande Troyen?

UYTDAGING (AEN M. D.)

Noch heb ick hert, al is my 't harnas-tuyg ontdragen,
    Een Rover uyt te dagen,
Die my, met schijn van deught, mijn wapens troonden af,
    Die ick hem willigh gaf,
En bood hem aen, dat ick 't geheim hem soud ontdecken,
    Om tot sijn eer te strecken.
Maer hoe! Een Hopman, hoe! een Kristen-Hertogh-heer,
    Geeft die geen leening weêr,
Onnosel afgeleent, en dat met smekend vleyen,
    Als Dalilas verleyen?
Weet, dat mijn kracht bestaet in geen locksoete tael,
    Maer in het vinnigh stael;

And you, helmeted maiden, loveliest of gods,
How could you let this happen, this conquering, this loss?
How could you let someone who's always honored you
Be brought so low, and by a child—a mere child!—too.
Each time this ill-born rascal sings his mother's praise
And slanders your great beauty I nearly burst with rage.
No, no, for me no body, whatever its repute,
Is lovely as a mind where virtue's taken root.
The shepherd who was sure his mother took the prize
Judged only by his lust—his choice was most unwise
In my esteem, for what was his reward, his gain?
The story ends, alas, in misery and pain.
Whose heart would not ward off each sweet flirtatious ploy
On seeing the sad waste of charred and ravaged Troy?

tr. Myra Scholz

MARIA TESSELSCHADE ROEMERS VISSCHER (1594–1649)

CHALLENGE (TO M. D.)*

Though stripped of armor, still I have the courage and belief
    To throw the gauntlet at the thief
Who, with seeming virtue, my arms from me extorted,
    Which willingly I would have him accorded
And granted him, and had I the secret to him disclosed
    So he would to honor'd glory be exposed.
But how! a captain, how! a Christian—leader—and grandee,
    Does he not return borrowed property,
Naively loaned, which he obtained with flattering implorations
    Much like Delilah's provocations?
Know that my powers don't rely on gentle coaxing of the ears,
    But on the sting of slender spears;

* Tesselschade wrote this playful letter to a captain (a certain M. D.) who, in the course of a flirtation, filched from her some intimate possession, perhaps a brooch. She plays with the imagery of the duel: the captain took her "armor," she can fight back with "steel." The reference here is to the steel needle used in the art of glass engraving, for which Tesselschade was famous. In this declaration of "war" she demands that the brooch be returned to her and insists that, in any case, it is not an emblem of her heart. Thus she delicately points out—in French—that she is not in love with the gentleman.

Dat dwing ick naer mijn sin; daer kan ick my me wreken,
　　In plaets van smijdigh smeken,
En segh hem oorlog aen die sachte vreede breeckt
　　En anders doet als spreeckt.
Ick sweer by 't snedigh stael, dat door kristal kan streven,
　　En Roemers brengt om 't leven,
Dat ghy my weder geeft, waar me ghy streefden deur
　　Ce qui n'est point mon Coeur.

AEN J. D. H.
Doen hij sijn Robijn voor mijn Diamant-Ringh wilde ruylen

Gy wenscht mijn Diamant met u Robijn te ruylen.
Wat hebt gy hier mee voor? Is 't insicht van gewin?
O neen, 'k geloof dat niet; hier speelt wat anders in.
Een schrand're minne-trek gaet sich hier onder schuylen.
Gy soekt door dese list te rechten Eere-zuylen,
En 't schitterige vyer van 't bloosende Robijn
Aan my te schenken, om my onder dese schijn
De herde Diamant en 't killig Ys 't ontschuylen.
Neen; 't Ys dat past my best, al valt het meenigh suur;
U borst, gelijk Robijn, een blaakend minne-vuur.
Een Minnaar moet geen smert noch ongemacken vreesen.
Als een Salmander moet hy onverteerbaar zijn,
En met standvastigheyd verdraagen wreede pijn.
Soo dwinght hy 't harde hert hem end'lijk te geneesen.

I bend those to my ways; and thus do I take my retaliation
    Rather than with wheedling speech make supplication;
And so I declare war on him who ruptures halcyon days,
    Who acts not according to what he says.
By etching steel that can cut crystal's edge,
    Can break glass goblets, I do take this pledge:
That you'll give back to me what you from me did plunder,
    Ce qui n'est point mon Coeur.[3]

                        tr. Marjolijn de Jager

KATHARINA QUESTIERS (1631 – 1669)

TO J. D. H.[4]
When he wanted to exchange his Ruby for my Diamond Ring

You wish to trade my diamond for your ruby?
What brings this on? The prospect of some gain?
No, that I don't believe. Another aim
Is lurking there, some love ploy hidden shrewdly.
You make this show of honor and entice
Me with your blushing ruby's brilliant flame
So you can pluck from me, as you would fain,
My hard-edged diamond and my chilly ice.
No; bitter though it seem, ice suits me best,
And you a fire blazing in your breast.
A lover must not fear distress or pain;
If, salamander-like, he shows no scorch
Of flames, but suffers steadfastly, he'll force
The heart that's hard to make him well again.

                        tr. Myra Scholz

AEN JUFR. CORNELIA VAN DER VEER
Op haer kouse-band die zij op mijn kamer had laaten leggen

Wou my de hulp-Goddin van 't groot Aegyptenlant
Zoo gunstig zyn als zy wel eertyds Iphis deede
Ik liet, spyt Engelland, een Waapen voor my smeeden
En wiert een Ridder van dees nieuwe Kousebant.

BRUIN BOVEN BLOND

Ruilt nooit uw verf, bevallige Bruinetten,
  Voor blanke kleur of blonde kuif.
De roos verbleekt voor bruine violetten,
  De witte wijkt de purpren druif.
De bloesemknop, zo teêr, zo ligt verstooven,
  Zwigt voor de rijpe kers in geur.
De staatige eik, hoe bruin van verw, praalt boven
  De taaije wilgen, wit van kleur.
Al wat natuur poogt kragten bij te zetten,
  Huldt ze altoos met een bruine huif.
Ruilt nooit uw verf, bevallige Bruinetten,
  Voor blanke kleur of blonde kuif.

TO MISS CORNELIA VAN DER VEER *
On finding the garter she left in my room

If Egypt's ancient goddess deigned to favor me
As long ago she granted Iphis's desperate plea,†
Then—England notwithstanding—I'd have a weapon made,
And "Knight of this New Garter" would be my accolade.‡

tr. Myra Scholz

ELISABETH KOOLAERT-HOOFMAN (1664—1736)

BETTER BROWN THAN BLONDE[6]

Don't ever change your color, fair brunettes,
   For lighter hue or blonder tress.
The rose looks pale beside dark violets,
   And white grapes never equal reds.
Sweet blossom fragrance, all too quickly gone,
   Gives way to cherries' full ripe scent.
The oak, so stately with its deep, rich crown
   Leaves willows looking wan and bent.
Whatever nature wishes to be strong
   She honors with dark hood or dress.
Don't ever change your color, fair brunettes,
   For lighter hue or blonder tress.

tr. Myra Scholz

---

* The poet Cornelia van der Veer was Questiers's bosom friend. Together they published the *Lauwerstryt (Praise Contest)* (1665), a collection of poems in which they competed in extolling each other. This poem is devoted to the garter which Cornelia, after her last visit, had left in Katharina's chamber, a detail that causes one to wonder about the nature of their relationship.

† Questiers, upon finding Cornelia's garter, wishes that the ancient Egyptian goddess Isis would change her into a boy. According to the story in Ovid's *Metamorphoses,* Iphis was born a girl but raised as a boy. Because her father had threatened to kill the child if it were a girl, Iphis's mother hid the true sex of her baby. When Iphis fell in love with the girl Ianthe, the parents arranged a wedding. Filled with both desire and a fear of detection, Iphis implored Isis to help her, and just before the wedding was changed into a beautiful young man.[5]

‡ As a nobleman the poet could have a weapon forged and become a Knight of Cornelia's Garter. She wants to do this England nothwithstanding. The Order of the Garter was an English institution, and at that time relations with England were strained. The poem was written during a truce in the war against England.

BESTENDIGHEID VAN 'T ONBESTENDIGE

Wat eertyds is gebeurd dat zienwe ook thans geschieden,
Eén zaak, op één tooneel, alleen door andre lieden.
Al 't geen de zon beschynt, al 't geen ons oog beschout,
Leert ons de wyste Vorst, is geenszins nieuw, maar oud:
Ofschoon de onweetendheid, als vreemd iets uit mag schreeuwen,
Dat zelfde is reeds geweest voor ons, in vroegere eeuwen.

Hoe dwaalt hy, die op de aarde een vast geluk verbeidt,
Daar niets bestendig is dan de onbestendigheid!

DE ONBESTENDIGHEID

Moest eindlijk Babijlon in puin en asch verkeeren,
 Die stad, die 't gansch Heeläl verwondring heeft gebaard!
 En gij, o Ninivé! dat zoo voortreflijk waart,
Kon niets den ondergang van uw Paleizen weeren?

Moest Titus Zegeboog zijn luister ook ontbeeren!
 Is Piza's heerlijk Beeld door de eeuwen niet gespaard!
 Ja, zag men 't woedend vuur, dien Tempel zoo vermaard,
Epheze's wonderstuk in eenen nacht verteeren!

 o Pharos! wierp de tijd uw trotsche vuurbaak neêr!
 Mauzool, is van uw Graf het minst bewijs niet meer!
In 't kort, kan niets op aard zijn eersten glans bewaaren?

 Wat reden heb ik dan om zoo verbaasd te staan,
Dat naa den trouwen dienst van acht of negen jaaren,
 Van mijn balijnenrok de haak is afgegaan?

DE VOLMAAKTE MAN

Gestadig in het werk tot nut van 't huisgezin,
 En ievrig om zijn ampt met glorie te bekleeden;
 Niet driftig, nooit geneigd tot wufte of dartle zeden;
Bezorgd voor zijn belang, maar wars van slecht gewin:

ZARA MARIA VAN ZON (?—1755)

CONSTANCY OF THE INCONSTANT

What's taken place before, we also see today,
All one affair, one stage, by different parties played.
All that the sun's rays shine on, all our eyes behold,
Teaches the wisest Lord, is not at all new, but old:
Though ignorance may loudly claim: here's something strange,
The same went long before us in a previous age.

Seeking steadfast happiness on earth's a fallacy,
As there is nothing constant but inconstancy!

tr. Wanda Boeke

JULIANA CORNELIA DE LANNOY (1738—1782)

INCONSTANCY

That Babylon should into dust and ash have receded,
　　The city that offered all the Universe delight!
　　And thou, O Nineveh, that was so fine a sight,
Could naught the downfall of your Palaces have impeded?

That Titus's Triumphal Arch of luster should be cheated!
　　And time grant Piza's lovely Image no respite!
　　Aye, some saw the raging fire consume o'ernight
Ephesos's masterpiece, that Temple once well-heeded!

　　O Pharos! down your proud fire beacon time did beat!
　　Mausolos, of your Grave th' effacement is complete!
In short, can naught on earth retain its newborn brightness?
　　What reason then have I to stand here well-nigh stunned
That after eight or nine years' dutiful uprightness
　　The hook to fasten my whalebone skirt has come undone?

tr. Wanda Boeke

THE PERFECT MAN

Constant in support of his family,
　　Plying his trade to make honor of it;
　　Never hasty, nor tending to frivolity;
Enterprising, but without false profit:

Aan 't spel niet toegedaan, aan Bacchus vocht nog min;
  Bedacht om zelfs met nut zijn' speeltijd te besteeden;
  Geen laf bewonderaar van vreemde aanvalligheden;
Verliefd, en tederlijk, maar op zijne Echtvrindin!

  Getrouw tot in den dood aan de eedle vriendschapsbanden;
  Bereid om voor den Staat zijn leeven te verpanden;
Meedogend, heusch, oprecht, wijs, vriendlijk, zacht van geest.

  De Man, met zooveel deugd, met zoo veel roem beschonken,
  Die Man, zoo dubbel waard in Dichtlust mij te ontvonken,
Is, naar ik merken kan, nog nooit op aard geweest.

LIJCAÖN

Dat andre Dichters vrij van Alexander zingen;
  Men heffe van Achill, of wel van Cesar aan:
  Ik doe die Helden recht, hun roem zal nooit vergaan,
Maar thans heeft eedler stof mijne ader doen ontspringen.

Ik zing den moedigsten van alle stervelingen.
  Ja dappre LIJAÖN, ik zal wat groots bestaan;
  Verrukt, verbaasd, bekoord, om duizend wonderdaân,
Zal ik uw' helden-kruin met eeuwig loof omringen.

  Meld dan mijn Zangeres, meld wat zijn arm bestond,
  Toen zich die andre Mars voor 't spits des Vijands vond,
Beziel mij, zo ik ooit uw' invloed heb genooten!

  Hoort Eeuwen! hij ontbloot zijn nooit verwonnen staal,
  Hij zwaait het om zijn hoofd tot zes of zevenmaal,
En . . . 'wel? wat deed hij toen?' 't is waarlijk mij ontschooten.

AAN DE HEEREN BESTUURDEREN DER
MAATSCHAPPIJ VAN DICHTKUNDE, TE 'S GRAVENHAGE
Bij gelegenheid mijner verkiezing tot Honnorair Lid

Beschermers van een Kunst die ieders hart bekoort,
Maar die zoo meenig nacht mij in mijn rust verstoort:
Is 't waarlijk uw besluit, en heb ik wel geleezen?
Ik zal dan Medelid van uw Genootschap weezen?
'k Beken, ik had die eer zoo streelend niet verwacht,
Nooit wierd ze aan mijne Sexe in Neêrland toegebragt.

No gambler he, no follower of Bacchus;
Eager to work every free day of his life;
Not prone to foreign charms that mock us;
Tender and loving, but only with his wife!

To noble friendships forever true;
To the State prepared to give life's due;
Kind, upright, wise, gentle from birth.

The man of such virtue, deserving renown,
That man, doubly blessed to inspire my poem,
Has, so to see, never walked on this earth.

tr. J. H. and J. W. Prins

LYCAON

Other poets the great Alexander have praised,
The wrath of Achilles, or Caesar their theme:
Those heroes I honor, their fame shall not fade,
But greater my own inspiration must seem.

I sing the most courageous of all mortal seed,
Yea dapper LYCAON, I'll make thee sublime,
Amazed and astonished at each marvelous deed,
I shall crown thy head with praise for all time.

Reveal then, my Muse, how he bravely faced death,
When he stood like Mars at th' Enemy's spear,
Inspire me, if ever I felt Muses' breath!

He bared his unvanquished steel, nobly begotten,
And brandished it six, seven times, O Centuries, hear!
And . . . "What did he do next?" In truth, I've forgotten.

tr. J. H. and J. W. Prins

TO THE GENTLEMEN OF THE BOARD OF THE POETRY SOCIETY IN THE HAGUE
On the Occasion of My Having Been Granted Honorary Membership

Patrons of the Art that charms the hearts of one and all,
But on so many a night has tortured me with its call,
Is it truly your decision and have I read it right?
That this Society of yours calls me to its ranks so bright?
Never dared I to aspire to thus become highly esteemed,
Never has my Sex in Holland been so honorably deemed.

Komt Dames, dankt mij vrij, gij kunt u billijk vleijên,
Dat ons dit goed begin wel verder heen zal leijên;
En ik bedrieg mij zeer, indien ons in het kort
De toegang tot den Raad ook niet ontslooten wordt:
De Pleitbank, 't Veld van Mars; onze eeuw is eens geboren.
Mijn Heeren, 'k zeg u dank voor de eer aan mij beschooren;
Ik neem die gretig aan, en vind me op 't hoogst gestreeld,
Dat ze in mijn Vaderland mij 't eerst wierd meêgedeeld.
　　Maar iets ontrust mij nog, ik wil 't u niet ontkennen,
Hoe zal ik 't Jufferschap aan deez mijn' eernaam wennen?
Ik had met zoo veel zorg mij naar den smaak geschikt,
Dat nooit de minste Vrouw van mij wierd afgeschrikt;
En wat ik aan mijn *Geest* ook eertijds heb geschreeven,
Men had mij naar het schijnt dat kortswijl lang vergeeven.
't Is waar, men beet wel eens elkandren in het oor,
Die Juffer die daar zit maakt vaerzen naar ik hoor:
Maar verder wierd mij zulks niet kwalijk afgenomen:
Doch nu, ik durf bijkans niet meer te voorschijn komen;
Mij dunkt men ziet mij reeds als van ter zijden aan,
En 'k zal bij elk gewis voor een *Savante* gaan.
En had ik maar alleen mijne eige Sex te vreezen,
Maar de uwe zal misschien niet min onreedlijk weezen.
Vergeefs betuig ik haar "Mijn Heeren, deeze smaak,
Die kunst die ge in ons doemt is waarlijk onze zaak;
Wij kunnen meerder zorg, meer tijd er aan besteeden.
Uw geest is meest bezet met nutter bezigheden;
Maar de onzen, bij geluk, zijn juist van zulk een' aart,
Dat elk die met gemak met deez verkiezing paart.
Wij maaken een ontwerp wijl we onze linten strikken,
En zulks belet ons niet om die met zwier te schikken:
'k Heb nooit zoo kloek 't *Beleg van Haarlem* voortgezet,
Dan als mij eenig Feest wat hield aan mijn *Toilet.*"
　　Maar kan 't vooroordeel ook naar goede reednen hooren?
Het best is dat we ons niet aan zijn berisping stooren.
Voor mij, 'k heb nu een steun, Mijn Heeren; ik vertrouw,
Zo mij de onweetendheid of de afgunst hoonen wou,
Dat gij voor de eer der Sex, en die der Kunst zoudt waaken,
En straks u van die zaak een *point d' honneur* zoudt maaken.
Der Muuzen Priesterschaar neemt wis tot hoofdwet aan,
Om waar het mooglijk zij de Dames voor te staan.

You may thank me, Ladies for you can all anticipate
That this start will lead us to a new victorious fate,
And I'd be surprised if we didn't soon gain access
To the innermost chambers of our Country's ruling Congress.
The Court of Law, the Game of War, our era has begun,
Gentlemen, receive my gratitude for the honor I have won.
I'm eager to accept it and am flattered to the core
That I'm the first Dutch lady for whom it lay in store.
    Yet one thing does still bother me, I surely won't deny,
How shall I accustom my sisters to this exceptional I?
I have done my best to conform to every woman's taste,
And never to offend even the most straitlaced;
For whatever I have written to the *Spirit* of my mind,*
I have long been forgiven, or so I now do find.
Verily the rumor ran its course from ear to ear,
That Lady there writes verses, verses, did you hear?
More serious objections were not wont to come my way,
But will I dare appear in public after this day?
I can feel in my direction the recent furtive looks,
Giving me the name of *Savant,* a Lady with her nose in books.
And it isn't my Sex only that I truly have to fear,
Yours too can be unreasonable and anything but clear.
To no avail I claim: "Dear Gentlemen, this flair
This Art that you deny to us is truly our affair!
We are the ones who care for it, we are the ones with time,
Your minds are concerned with matters more urgent than rhyme.
But our chores are such, by virtue of their nature,
That we can easily combine them with this honorary stature.
We design our plots in the course of a sewing session,
Which never has prevented us from keeping pace with fashion.
Never did the *Battle of Haarlem* ascend to such great splendor
As when I prettied myself and colored my cheeks so tender."
    But can prejudice listen to reason and common sense?
Let us be deaf to its reproaches and never take offense.
For your support is mine now, dear Gentlemen, I trust,
If I am mocked by ignorance, you are the ones who must
Guard the honor of the female and of the finest Art,
And make it a *point d'honneur* now and ever in your heart.
The Clergy of the Muses will take as guiding light,
The task of doing for the Ladies all that's in their might.

---

* Refers to an earlier feminist poem by de Lannoy, "Aan mij geest" ("To My Spirit").

Wel aan, 'k zal dan Pegaaz op nieuws de sporen geeven,
En in ons roemrijk perk naar versche lauwren streeven.
Maar zult ge inschiklijk zijn, Kunstbroederen? 't belge u niet,
Indien ge mij zomtijds, wat lang verpoozen ziet.
Hoe zeer ik naar de gunst der Muuzen ook mag dingen,
't Was nimmer mijn gewoonte om haar iets af te dwingen:
En 'k vleij mij, dat ik meer voor onze zaak verricht,
Wanneer ik eens in 't jaar met smaak een vierling dicht;
Dan dat ik reis op reis, door iedlen waan gedreeven,
Een boekdeel saamenstel met geest noch zwier geschreeven.
Apol roept ons niet toe "schrijft Dichtren, 'k geef u taak:"
Maar zegt ons "doet uw best, men leest u voor vermaak."
O Rampspoed voor een kunst, der Wijzen kunst voor deezen!
Schier elk die leezen kan wil thans een dichter weezen:
En als die drift eens werkt en plaats grijpt in het bloed,
Is 't of men op den hals gestadig rijmen moet:

Mijn Heeren, laat ons niet in die verkeerdheid geeven,
Maar liever minder doen en naar 't volmaakte streeven:
Zingt weinig Dichtren-reij, maar zingt verrukkend schoon,
Zo vlecht u ganssh Europe een cierlijke Eerekroon.
    Maar ben ik wel bedacht om zelf dit naa te komen,
En zal 't mij mogelijk zijn mijn iever in te toomen?
Ik zwijgen, ik alleen, daar elk de snaren spant!
Beminnaars van de kunst, neemt vrij de lier ter hand,
Thans kunt ge in ons gewest op schoone lauwren hoopen;
Het edelst glorieperk gaat eindlijk voor ons open:
Wij zingen om den Prijs, het oogenblik genaakt,
Waar in een grootsche zege uw' naam onsterfelijk maakt.
'k Bedrieg me, of 'k zie 't vernuft, roemwaarde Kunstmeceenen,
Thans met vernieuwden moed zijn lust en vlijt verêenen.
Voor mij, 't is u bekend wat ik op Pindus doe;
Ik wijde *Melpomeen* voor lang mijn pooging toe.
Doch hoe ook haar belang mij steeds aan 't hart zal raaken,
'k Zal trachten op mijn beurt bij u mijn hof te maaken.
Ik voel voor 't Hekeldicht zomtijds een weinig trek;
En als ik in een vrind iets tegen de orde ontdek,
't Zij kleeding, zwier of tred, van kwaaden smaak moog weezen,
Hij mag gelijk *van Ghert* mijne eerste dichtluim vreezen:
Ja menig daagt mij uit, en vordert als een gunst,
Dat ik zijn feilen kies tot voorwerp van mijn kunst.

Into the flanks of Pegasus again my spurs will sink,
Distinction of new laurels will spring from female ink.
Bear with me, fellow poets, and do not be disturbed,
If at some place I dwell too long, you shouldn't be perturbed.
No matter what I do to court the Muses' favor,
I never tried to force them or tell them whom to savor.
I think a single verse would be better for our cause,
A fine line once a year giving reason for pause
Than time after time, as a slave to Vanity,
A new and mindless volume filled with mere inanity.
Apollo never summons us, "Your task, poets, is to write,"
But says, "Your only task should be to give the world delight."
Oh, woe for a noble Art, once only the wisest could know it,
That every soul who now can read does think himself a poet.
And once the urge has caught him, flows through all his veins
The drive to rhyme does paralyze and thus defies all pains.

Dear Gentlemen, let us do right and let's not go astray,
But rather produce less and seek the perfect way.
Sing verses few in number but of exquisite sheen,
And so weave a crown for Europe, quite worthy of a Queen.
  But do I have the gift to follow all these rules?
At length to curb my zeal, to use the proper tools?
Shall I be silent? I alone? when all pour out their heart?
Wax lyrical, play on, oh lovers of the Art!
Crowns of laurel are here for us who do aspire,
The era of glory has come to this our noble shire.
We are singing for the Prize, the moment has come nigh,
When the grandest victory will ring your name on high.
With courage now reborn, I see the finest ingenuity,
Unite its joy and diligence to form a new congruity.
It might be clear, Maecenases, what in essence I do.
To *Melpomene* I have long been a real devotee true.
No matter how my love of Her might move my tender heart,
It is among your choir I hope to stand and sing my part.
Lampoonery is my weak spot and yours I'd love to see,
An arrow to Achilles' heel is a pleasure to set free.
If ever friend or enemy shows abominable taste,
To point it out, as with *van Ghert,* I surely would make haste.*
Yes many have defied me to favor them with wit,
To etch their faults in poems as sharply as I see fit.

---

* Refers to an earlier satirical poem on a certain Mr. van Ghert.

Dus hoop ik binnen kort in rijm en maat te krijgen,
Hoe zeker geestlijk Heer, wiens naam ik nu zal zwijgen,
Maar die mij zedert lang om een *satire* plaagt,
Wel tien Japonnen heeft en iedle muilen draagt.
   Mijn Heeren, 't spijt mij zeer, 'k ben hier wat afgelegen,
En op wat wijze ik ook de zaak mooge overweegen,
De zedigheid, wier wet ik billijk hulde doe,
Laat mij vooreerst nog niet in uw vergadring toe:
Maar kunt ge mij geen lijst van uw gebreken zenden?
't Waar immers op zijn plaats dat wij elkandren kenden.
Ik kon dan in die stof vast weiden naar mijn zin,
En zag voor u en mij daar niets dan voordeel in.
   Maar wat stoutmoedigheid! zult ge immer die verschoonen?
Een ander zingt misschien uw lof op hooge toonen;
Verheft met eedlen zwier, hoe groots gij t' samen spant,
Ter glorie van de Kunst en die van 't Vaderland.
Wat konde ik niet tot roem van uw Beschermers zeggen!
'k Moest hun grootmoedigheid hier duidlijk openleggen;
Het voordeel gelden doen dat ge uit hun pooging wacht,
En de eer die hun verbeidt bij 't kunstrijk Nageslacht:

En daar ik een ontwerp zoo luisterrijk laat steeken,
Verzoek ik voor begin een lijst van uw gebreeken.
't Is waarlijk fraai bedacht om in uw gunst te staan,
En mooglijk schrapt ge mij eer ik aan 't werk kan gaan.
Maar 'k bid u, laat de pen u niet te ras ontglijen,
Mijn Zangster zal misschien zich naar de reden vleijen:
Of neemt ze eens bij geval de proef van uw geduld,
'k Beloof u dat ge er zelf het eerst om lachen zult.

AAN MEJUFFROUW AGATHA DEKEN

   Ach DEKEN! DEKEN, ach! myn waarde WOLFF! myn man!—
In 't holst des nachts!—'k zit voor zyn ledikant te leezen;
   Hy spreekt met my, hy sterft, valt in myn' arm!—ik kan
Niet schryven!—hemel! moest ik juist alleenig weezen!

I therefore hope that soon I'll rhyme and measure out,
How a certain pious gentleman, whose name we'll do without,
But who has long been yearning for a satire from my pen,
Wears robes of silk and velvet as his frivolous secret yen.

    Gentlemen, I trust you will excuse me my digressing,
No matter how I ponder it: this subject is most pressing,
Decency, the rules of which I willingly obey,
Does bar me from your meeting, or so it be today.
But can you not disclose to me your heart's most shameful delights?
Isn't getting to know each other one of the noblest birthrights?
I would then happily roam at will in the pastures of your stories,
For you and me this would produce a multitude of glories.

    My Lord! Good Heavens! How dare I! Will you ever forgive me?
Another might sing your praise in eternal jubilee,
And elevate with splendor your brotherly conjunction,
To hail Art and the Fatherland and serve a noble function.
To the honor of your Patrons what an Ode would I devote,
And all their generosity and magnificence I would note.
Each word would add a stitch to the pattern of their fame,
And adorn forever the grandeur of both our names.

But as I have abandoned a plan so very becoming,
I'd like to have a list of your every shortcoming.
Wouldn't this pave my way into your lyric heart?
Or will you scratch me from your books before I even start?
I beg you take your time before you dip your pen,
Reason may temper my Muse and my tongue every now and then.
And even if your patience sometimes is abused,
I promise you with all my heart, you shall first be amused.

       tr. Sheila Gogol and Erica Eijsker

ELIZABETH WOLFF-BEKKER (1738–1804)

TO MISS AGATHA DEKEN *

    Ah DEKEN! DEKEN! oh! my worthy WOLFF! My husband!—
In the depths of the night!—I sit and read beside his bed;
    He speaks to me, he dies, falls into my arms!—I can
Not write!—O Heaven! alone and at this hour!

---

* Betje Wolff-Bekker addressed this poem to Agatha Deken, with whom she shared most
of her life.[7]

Geen ziekte, zelfs geen koorts; zo zegt hy nog: *'k Ben wèl;*
Slechts wat vermoeid; dit komt van gisteren te preêken:
    Myn lief, 'k word wat benaauwd—hy richt zig op—'k ontstel;
'k Vlieg op—hy zwygt, hy geeft een snik—zyne oogen breeken;
    Zyn hoofd zygt op mijn hart—hy ziet my stervende aan:
"Myn lieve waarde WOLFF!"—afgryslyke oogenblikken!
    "Ach! kent gy my niet meer? ik ben 't:" het was gedaan.
Denk, denk eens myn vriendin! hoe dit my heeft doen schrikken!
    'k Ben byna levenloos! (gy kent myn teder hart:)
Ach, niemand spreekt my toe! geen maagschap, geene vrinden!
    Ik schryf 't, ik klaag 't aan u—wat is myn geest verward!
Ja! dit's het doodsgewaad; daarin zult gy hem vinden.
    Geheel alleen!—wat zal ik doen? wie geeft my raad?
'k Moet van dit sterfgeval noodzaaklyk kennis geeven:
    Ja, 'k moet; maar vinde my hiertoe gantsch buiten staat:
Hoe zal dat gaan? zie, hoe myn zwakke vingren beeven:
    Ik schryf onleesbaar schrift: vriendin! wie staat my by?
Wie helpt, wie troost my? ach! myn waardste DEKEN! gy.

In de Beemster, 29 April 's nachts,
ten 1 uure, MDCCLXXVII

VRIENDSCHAPSZUCHT

    Gy die de zielen vormde, en elk haare egaê gaf!
Mag ik die hemelgift, myn Zielsvriendin! niet minnen? . . .
Wat valt het leeven van trouwhartige Vriendinnen,
    Als zy gescheiden zyn niet bitter, hard en straf!
    Ik min haar als my-zelf, ja 'k min haar al zo teêr:
Dan ach! naauw zie ik haar, of moet haar weêr begeeven!
Laat my toch, 't gaa hoe 't gaa, met mijn MARIA leeven!
    Gun my dees bede, ô Vriend der Vrienden! 'k wensch
    niet meer.

No illness, not a sign of fever, but one moment he said: *I am well,*
Just somewhat tired, from preaching yesterday,
  My love, the air constricts me somewhat—he sits up—I am aghast,
I jump up from my place—he keeps his silence, then a sob—his eyes break,
  His head sinks on my heart—dying he gazes at me,
"My sweet worthy WOLFF!"—such horrible moments!
  "Ah! knowst thou me no more? 'tis I." And all was done.
Imagine, oh imagine, my friend! how this did frighten me!
  Almost lifeless am I! (thou knowest the tenderness of my heart).
Ah, no one to address me! nor kith nor kin, nor friends!
  I write these lines, to you I 'plain—how confusion in my mind does
  reign!
Yes! This is the shroud, in which you will find him.
  Solitary and alone!—what am I to do? who is to counsel me?
Of this decease I must needs give account,
  Yes, I must, but am of such account not capable,
How will it be? See, how my weak fingers tremble,
  My writing runs illegibly. Friend! who is there to stand by me?
Who can help, who can console? Ah! my worthy DEKEN! Thee.

In the Beemster, April 29th at night,
at 1 o'clock, MDCCLXXVII

tr. Tony Briggs

AGATHA DEKEN (1741–1804)

LOVE OF FRIENDSHIP

Thou shaper of souls, that gave to each her own!
May I not love as Heaven's gift, my soul's companion? . . .
Oh, the life of women friends who are parted
Is cruel, bitter, and broken-hearted!
I love her as myself, yes I love her tenderly,
Then alas! I barely saw her, who must leave me!
Let me live with my MARIA, as well I may,
I'll wish no more, O Friend of Friends, to whom I pray.

tr. J. H. and J. W. Prins

GRAFSCHRIFT OP ROBESPIERRE

Stort hier geen tranen, wandelaar!
  Om dat hy de oogen sloot;
Want zoo hy nog in 't leven waar'
  Dan waart gy zeker dood!

  Passant, ne pleure pas son sort
  Car, s'il vivait, tu serais mort.

OP HET AFSTERVEN VAN ONS DERDE DOCHTERTJEN, ADELHEIDE IRENE, NAAR HAAR TWEE OVERLEDEN ZUSJENS, GENOEMD

Lief wichtj', in wie IRENE, in wie de teedre AÂLEIDE,
  Het bloedend oudrenhart te rug gegeven scheen,
Wat hijgde ik naar de troost die me uw geboort' bereidde!
  Helaas! zy was me op nieuw de voorbô van geween.
Viooltjen van den hof, bewaakt door Cherubijnen,
  Gy waart geen moederborst bestemd tot pronksieraad!
Ik zag de leliebloem, en 't roosjen meê, verdwijnen,
  Dat thands, volmaakt in bloei, in 's Heilands kweekhof staat.
Ga, paar gy met die twee, paar met uw drietal broederen,
  In schaduw van Gods throon voor de eeuwigheid gekweekt;
Eens prijke ik weêr met u, de zaligste aller moederen,
  Wanneer de nacht van 't graf voor 't jongste daglicht breekt!

[EENS DANSTE IK IN EEN CSÁRDA]
Aan Sebestyén

Eens danste ik in een Csárda,
Op de Puszta te Hortobágy.

De muziek klonk wild, mijn hartstocht steeg
In de Csárda op de Puszta te Hortobágy.

KATHARINA WILHELMINA BILDERDIJK-SCHWEICKHARDT (1777—1830)

EPITAPH FOR ROBESPIERRE

Weep here no tears for him who died,
   I say to you who here do tread,
For should he now still be alive
   You surely would be dead!

Passant, ne pleure pas son sort
Car, s'il vivait, tu serais mort.

   tr. Sheila Gogol and Erica Eijsker

AT THE PASSING AWAY OF OUR THIRD DAUGHTER, ADELHEIDE IRENE, NAMED AFTER HER TWO DECEASED SISTERS

Sweet baby girl, in whom IRENE, in whom the gentle AÂLEIDE,
   Seemed restored to their bleeding parents' hearts,
How did I yearn for the solace of your birth!
   Alas! To me it was the herald of new tears.
Little violet in bud, watched by cherubim,
   Not fated to adorn a joyful mother's breast!
I saw the lily disappear and the rose as well,
   In perfect bloom they now grace the Savior's Garden.
Unite with both of them and with your three dear brothers,
   In the shadow of God's throne, bred for all eternity,
One day I'll show you off again, the most blissful of mothers,
   When the grave's night dawns on Judgment Day!

   tr. Sheila Gogol and Erica Eijsker

GIZA RITSCHL (1869—1942)

[ONCE I DANCED IN A CSÁRDA]
To Sebestyén

Once I danced in a Csárda,
On the Puszta in Hortobágy.

The music was wild, my feelings caught fire
In the Csárda on the Puszta in Hortobágy.

De glazen rinkelden, wijn en passie maakten mij dronken
In de Csárda op de Puszta te Hortobágy.

En o, wel duizend liedjes klonken
In de Csárda op de Puszta te Hortobágy.

Nu zit ik hier en droom
Van de Puszta te Hortobágy.

En telkens welt in mij op het schoone,
Van de Puszta te Hortobágy.

In een Fata Morgana zweeft mijn gedachte
Naar U, mijn Puszta te Hortobágy.

En naar de lieve Csárda waarin ik danste en lachte
Op de Puszta te Hortobágy.

[IK WÌL NIET MEER ALS VROEGER TOT U GAAN]

Ik wìl niet meer als vroeger tot U gaan;
Ik kàn niet meer als immer met U spreken
Van dit, en dat—klein-woordjes oversteken
Van twee, die niet de zelfde taal verstaan.

Zal ik dan nòoit den dunnen ijskorst breken,
Waarop mijn arme handen machtloos slaan?
—Zie niet zoo laag: ge zult me nòoit zien staan
Als ge zóó laag ziet: 'k stà niet laag, en 'k reken

Mij tot uw Volk.—Nu wil ik voortaan vrij
Kome' in uw huis—als broeder, nieuw-gevonden,

Aanzitten aan dezèlfde tafelronde,
En breken van hetzèlfde brood als gij;

En 't kruim,—geef dàt gerustlijk aan de honden
Want kruim, dat 's hondenspijs; gèen spijs voor mìj!

The glasses rang out, passion and wine made me drunk
In the Csárda on the Puszta in Hortobágy.

And oh, a thousand songs must have echoed
In the Csárda on the Puszta in Hortobágy.

Now I sit here and dream
Of the Puszta in Hortobágy.

Again and again all the beauty floods back
Of the Puszta in Hortobágy.

In a Fata Morgana my thoughts float over
To you, my Puszta in Hortobágy.

And to the Csárda I love, that I danced in, laughing,
On the Puszta in Hortobágy.

tr. Myra Scholz

HENRIETTE ROLAND HOLST-VAN DER SCHALK (1869–1952)

[I DO NOT WANT TO MEET YOU AS BEFORE]

I do not want to meet you as before;
I cannot speak to you as I have anymore
Of this and that—passing civilities
Of two who don't understand the same tongue.

Shall I never break the crust of ice so thin
That I strike at with my hands in vain?
—Do not look far down: you will not see me
If you look that low: I am not far below and I remain

One of your People.—From now on I will freely
Come into your house—as a brother, newly found,

Share the same table round
And break the same bread as you;

And the crumbs—give them to your hounds
For crumbs are food for dogs: I sweep them to the ground!

tr. Ria Loohuizen

OVER HET ONTWAKEN MIJNER ZIEL

De volle dagen komen met bedaarde
stappen schrijdend, als hooge witte vrouwen
uit tooversprooken: bloem in handen houen
ze en licht is om hun hoofden, goud-behaarde.
De dagen liggen open als verklaarde
geheimen tusschen vrienden die 't lang wouen
zeggen en zwegen, lang: tot hun vertrouwen
vol-groeid was en elk zijn ziel openbaarde.

Dagen als bloemen, open-volle nachten
daartusschen, als in maanlicht blanke tuinen
en midden tusschen deze vele ga ik
met stralende oogen levens-op. Nu sta ik
me dunkt, als opperste van rijen duinen
en zie wijd weg: dit is het lang-verwachte.

MOEDER VAN VISSCHERS
bij een teekening

Zie mij: mijn mond verleerde vroeg te klagen
mijn oog is strak gelijk een winternacht,
berusting heeft mij jong den staf gebracht
waarmee ik klim naar het eind mijner dagen.

Ik ken geen hoop, ik heb nooit iets verwacht;
zonen en doch'tren baarde ik om te dragen
wat ik zelf draag; toen z' onder 't hart mij lagen
heb ik, om hunnentwil, veel droefs gedacht.

Soms groeit iets in mij op in grim'ge nachten
wanneer mijn zonen huiv're' op barre zee
maar daagt de morgen, ben ik het vergeten;

dan is mij of hun jonge hoofde' iets weten
te blij voor mij, of die hooplooze vreê
met mij gaat sterven en dat niets-verwachten.

MY SOUL'S AWAKENING

And now the full days come, with calm
steps striding like tall white women
from fairy tales, with flowers in their hands
and light around their heads of golden hair.
The days lie open like secrets
shared at last among friends who long wanted
to speak and long were silent until their trust
ripened and each could reveal his soul.

Days like flowers, nights full and open
in between as in gardens white with moonlight
and I in their midst walking toward life
against the current and standing now
I think the highest in a row of dunes
and looking out: this is the long awaited.

tr. Andre Lefevere

MOTHER OF FISHERMEN
on a drawing

Look at me: my mouth soon learned not to complain,
my eyes are hard as winter nights,
resignation early brought me the staff
I lean on to climb to the end of my days.

I know no hope, I had no expectations,
I bore sons and daughters to bear what I have borne
and when they lay under my heart
my thoughts were often sad for their sake.

At times something new grows in me on grim nights
when my sons stand shuddering on the barren sea
but I have forgotten it when morning comes

and it seems as if their young heads might know
too much joy for me, as if that hopeless peace
and all I do not expect will cease with me.

tr. Andre Lefevere

WISSENBOS

Hier roept de tortel, de fazant;
het waterhoen heeft 't nest geplant
tussen de wissen en het riet.
Een sperwer schreeuwt. Gij ziet hem niet
maar in 't nabije stoppelveld
heeft hij zijn nieuwe prooi geteld.

Het ruikt naar munt, naar wilde tijm.
Een spin kleeft aan de vogellijm;
ik ril en plooi de takken om . . .
Waar is het pad dat ik beklom?

Duizenden wissen binden mij
aan deze grond, aan u. En gij
die zoekt hoe men de pijn, de tijd
kan zalven, zonder bitterheid,
geef mij de hand, breng mij terug . . .

Tussen de wilgen breekt een brug . . .

Ik vrees 'k word eens die vreemde vrouw
die langs 't moeras de nacht in wou . . .

A LA OMAR KHAYYAM

Wat al mijn geest uit vriendschap wint,
de liefste is mij liever dan de vrind.
Het leven, als mysterie met den vrind besproken
is mij thans met de liefste raadselloos ontloken.

JULIA TULKENS (1902)

WILLOW-WOOD

Here turtledoves and pheasants call;
between the willows and the sprawl
of reed the moorhen's lodged a nest.
A hawk cries out, you know the rest
though it's unseen—new prey will yield
in stubble of a nearby field.

There's smell of mint, of wild thyme.
A spider sticks to fresh birdlime;
I tremble, bend the branches down . . .
The path I came on, is it gone?

A thousand osiers bind me to
this ground, bind me to you. And you
who seek a salve for pain, for time,
that leaves no bitterness behind,
give me your hand and lead me back . . .

Through leaves a bridge breaks on the track . . .

Someday I'll be as strange, I fear,
as she who longed to disappear
on swampy paths into the night . . .

      tr. Myra Scholz

ANNA BLAMAN (1905–1960)

A LA OMAR KHAYYAM *

Whatever my spirit from friendship gains,
more beloved than a friend my dearest love remains.
Life, discussed as mystery with friends,
has blossomed with my love to bring the riddle's end.

      tr. Marjolijn de Jager

---

* Omar Khayyam was a Persian poet (born ca. 1050) who constructed the Eastern quatrain: a four-line serious poem containing a striking piece of wisdom about life. His famous classical collection of quatrains is called *The Rubaiyat.*

DANS

Ik omvat met bei mijn armen de tere ronding
van haar schouders en hals, en zijzelve
doet mij haar zachtglooiende dansende benen omhelzen
zo schrijden wij tezamen in rhythmische wiegeling

Ik zie omhooggeheven haar lief gezicht
en dit hevig bijeenzijn drijft mij dicht
en dichter tot haar—en wij dansen mond aan mond
en hart aan hart en zacht gezicht aan zacht gezicht

BIOGRAFISCH

De taal slaapt in een syllabe
en zoekt moedergrond om te aarden.

Vijf jaren is oud genoeg.
Toen mijn vader, die ik het vroeg,

mij zeide: "dat is een grondel,"
—en ik zag hem, zwart in de sloot—

legde hij het woord in mij te vondeling,
open en bloot.

Waarvoor ik moest zorgen,
met mijn leven moest borgen:

tot aan mijn dood.

DANCE

With my two arms I hold the tender circle
of her shoulders and her neck, and she
she makes me hug the soft hills of her dancing legs
and so we stride together in a rhythmic rocking

I see her sweet face raised high
and this fierce communion drives me near
and nearer to her—and we are dancing mouth to mouth
and heart to heart and gentle face to gentle face

tr. Marjolijn de Jager

IDA GERHARDT (1905–1997)

BIOGRAPHICAL

Language sleeps in a syllable
and seeks root in mother soil.

Five years is old enough.
When my father, whom I asked,

told me: "that's a groundling,"
—and I saw it, black in the ditch—

he placed the word in me, a foundling,
open and bare.

which I would have to nurture,
protect with my life,

until my death.

tr. J. H. and J. W. Prins

DE RATTEN

's Nachts hoorden wij in 't holle huis
de ratten rennen langs de binten.
Zij scheurden spaanders van de plinten;
in kasten viel de kalk tot gruis.

De Rotte gistte van bederf.—
Uw fierheid heeft geen kamp gegeven:
ge hebt het vaal gespuis verdreven,
nòg: de boerin op eigen erf.

Maar later, 's nachts in het gewelf
der kelders hoorden wij u vloeken;
uw bezem bonkte—in lege hoeken:
De ratten zaten in uzelf.

VOOR M. VASALIS

Soms lijken uw verzen uit oerleem,
een aarde zwaar van gehalte,
nog vochtig van wegtrekkend water.
Het leem van de eerste mens Adam.

Soms naderen zij mij als nevelen,
damp van de waterwoestijnen
des aanvangs. Het raam van mijn kamer
wordt wit; er is mist aan mijn haren.

En soms zijn zij adem en windvlaag.

Maar mijn tranen zijn om die enkele
die ontstijgen alreeds bij de aanhef.
De ontzegden: óók aan uzelve.
Zij vinden hun weg naar de sterren.

THE RATS

At night inside the hollow house,
we heard the rats below the floor.
They tore off splinters from the beams,
the plaster in closets crumbled to dust.

The Rotte River foamed with decay.—
Relentless, you would not give in.
You drove the foul creatures away;
a farmer's wife, you held your ground.

But late at night we heard your curses
somewhere deep down in the cellar;
your broom pounded—in empty corners:
The rats were hidden in yourself.

> *tr. J. H. and J. W. Prins*

TO M. VASALIS *

Sometimes your verses seem of primal clay,
of marled and heavy earth,
still moist from ebbing water.
Clay of Adam, the first human.

Sometimes they approach like wisps of fog,
vapor from the watery wastes
of the beginning. The window in my room
turns white; there is mist on my hair.

And sometimes they are breath and gust of wind.

My tears though are for those few
that rise from the very start.
The ones denied us and even you.
They find their way to the stars.

> *tr. J. H. and J. W. Prins*

* M. Vasalis is one of the most important female poets of the Netherlands. She has a small oeuvre but an enormous influence. She is Gerhardt's contemporary.

ARCHAÏSCHE GRAFSTEEN

In het verscholen thijmdal,
domein der honingbijen,
de dodensteen, de stèlè.
"Mètoon wijdt deze grafsteen
aan zijn verkoren Aktè,
de moeder zijner zonen,
die stierf, oud twintig jaren.
Zij heeft het brood gebakken,
zij heeft de wol gesponnen,
het huis in stand gehouden."
De wind beweegt, de bijen
zoemen de stilte stiller;
zij arbeiden, zij fluisteren:
"het huis in stand gehouden,
het huis in stand gehouden."

SAPPHO

Schoon gelaat, van droppels nog overfonkeld,
trotse tranen om het volmaakt geboren
strofisch lied dat, jong aan het licht gesprongen,
opent de ogen.

Dit uw dracht van brandingomvlaagde dagen,
nachten dat gij slapeloos weer der sterren
straling zag vergaan, als het klare maanlicht
alschijnend opkomt.

Wie kan leed u doen?—Aan de strofen ontstijgen
zeedoorwaaide geuren van thijm en bijen,
ook het openkomen der grote rozen
nimmer genaderd.

ARCHAIC GRAVESTONE

In the hidden thyme valley,
domain of honey bees,
the tombstone, the stele.
"Mètoon dedicates this stone
to Aktè his chosen one
the mother of his son,
who died at twenty years.
She baked the bread,
she spun the wool,
kept the house together."
The wind stirs, the bees
hum the quiet into silence;
they work, they whisper:
"kept the house together,
kept the house together."

tr. J. H. and J. W. Prins

SAPPHO

Fairest face, still glazed with the sparkling teardrops
shed in pride for verses just born, for perfect
strophic song that now, newly sprung to light, is
opening eyes.

This the fruit you carried through surging-surf-filled
days and sleepless nights, when you saw how radiant
stars grow dim again, as the moon ascends with
all-shining light.

Who can harm you now? From the strophes rise fresh
sea-blown breezes fragrant with thyme and bees, and
with that slow unfolding of large-bloomed roses
never nearby.

tr. Myra Scholz

DE HEKS

Ga haar niet achteloos voorbij,
Zij, die de lage werken doet,
Den vloer schrobt en de netten boet,
Het hoofd buigt over huisgerei.

Wie zal u zeggen of haar geest
Eenstemmig met haar handen leeft,
Waar in haar oog nog smeulend beeft
De nagloed van een heidensch feest.

Wellicht dat om haar slapen sloot
Een lang vergeten koningskroon,
Of eerder was z'in bosch en vroon
Pans metgezel en jachtgenoot.

ERWTJES

Toen ze een meisje was van zeventien
moest ze een hele middag erwtjes doppen
op het balkon. Ze wou de teil omschoppen.
Ze was heel woest. Ze kon geen erwt meer zien.

Teon ging ze maar wat dromen, van geluk,
en dat geluk had niets te doen met erwten
maar met de Liefde en de Grote Verte.
Dat dromen hielp. Het scheelde heus een stuk.

En dat is meer dan vijftig jaar terug.
Ze is nu zeventig en heel erg fit.
En altijd als ze 's middags even zit,
mijmert ze, met een kussen in de rug,

over geluk en zo . . . een beetje warrig,
maar het heeft niets te maken met de Verte
en met de Liefde ook niet. Wel met erwten,
die komen altijd weer terug, halsstarrig.

CLARA EGGINK (1906–1991)

THE WITCH

Don't pass her by without a glance,
She who performs such menial chores
As mending nets and scrubbing floors
And bending over pots and pans.

Who says her spirit and her hands
Have learned to live in harmony?
Still smoldering in her eyes you see
The embers of a heathen dance.

In times no memory can scan
She may have worn some royal crown
Or stalked through forest, grove and down
On hidden hunting paths with Pan.

tr. Myra Scholz

ANNIE M. G. SCHMIDT (1911–1995)

PEAS

One afternoon, when still in her teens,
shelling green peas on a balcony,
she fell into a rage, couldn't stand another pea.
Felt like kicking the pail to smithereens.

Then she began dreaming of joy and wonder
of everything the peas were not.
Dreaming helped. It helped a lot.
She dreamed of Love and the Great Blue Yonder.

That was more than fifty years ago.
Now she is seventy and very fit.
Every afternoon she finds time to sit
And muse, propped up by a pillow,

about joy and such . . . a little confused,
but not about the Blue Yonder or Love.
It's the peas she can't let go of.
They won't go away. They simply refuse.

Ach ja, zegt ze. Ik kan mezelf nog zien,
daar in mijn moeders huis op het balkon,
bezig met erwtjes doppen in de zon.
Dat was geluk. Toen was ik zeventien.

MOEDER DICHT

Mijn bladerloze schaduw mijdt het water
Ziezo hè hè, de eerste regel staat er.
en speurt de witte angst van eeuwen later
Ga weg! Ga spelen met je transformator!
Je ziet toch dat je moeder zit te dichten.
ik wend mij af en doof mijn vale lichten
ik heb tedúm tedúm tedúm *geweten*
Dat vul ik later in. Na 't middageten.
mijn weemoed maakt de koele vlinders wakker
van mijn getooide zelf. Daar is de bakker!
Zeg maar: een halfje bruin en een heel wit.
o grijze schim, die daar zo heilloos zit
ik zie mijn grijze droefheid aan de kim
Da's tweemaal grijs. Dat kan niet. *naakte schim*
aan wie ik al mijn zachte treurnis zeg
En nog een rol beschuit! O is ie weg?
als dauw die druppelt van de trage bomen
Als jij nog één keer binnen durft te komen,
dan krijg je geen vanillevla vanavond!
zo druppelt in dit hart te zeer gehavend
Je moeder dicht. Ze heeft geen tijd, totaal niet.
Als vader thuiskomt gaat het helemaal niet.
Je moeder zou een Shakespeare kunnen zijn.
Ze is het niet. Dat komt door jouw gedrein.
Daar gaat ie weer. *O humtum klaar en koel*
in 't land van late regen en ik voel
mijn schamelheid. Een heer met een kwitantie?
Zeg maar: m'n moeder is met kerstvakantie.
mijn schamelheid. Wat is dat? Hoofdje zeer?
M'n schatje toch . . . Gevallen met je beer?
Je moeder komt . . . na na . . . daar is ze al.
Wees nou maar zoet—'t genie staat weer op stal.

Ah yes, she says. My mother's balcony,
I can still see it now, how I sat
in the sun at age seventeen and that
was bliss, shelling pea after pea after pea.

tr. J. H. and J. W. Prins

MOTHER MUSING

My leafless shadow shuns the water
Thank God, the first line finally got there.
and smells the blanched fear of later centuries
Get out! Go play with your transformer, please!
You know your mother's busy with the muse.
I turn aside, my light has lost its hues
and (something something) *I have known*
I'll complete that later, this afternoon.
My melancholy stirs the chrysalis
of my perfected self. The baker—there he is!
Tell him: one half wheat and one whole white.
O shadow gray, devoid of light
on the horizon I spy my gray sorrow
That's twice gray. Let's try *O naked shadow*
I confide my soft sadness to you alone
And ask him for some crackers! Oh, has he gone?
as with dreary trees that shed their dew
Come once more in this room and you are through!
And no vanilla pudding for you tonight!
so this heart weeps its painful plight
Your mother is inspired and needs to be clearheaded.
No time! Once your father comes home, forget it.
Your mother could have been another Shakespeare.
She is not. Thanks to your whining, my dear.
Here we go again. *O* (something) *clear and real*
in this land of rain and mist I feel
my poverty. A man with bills to pay?
Tell him your mother went on holiday.
my poverty. What now? Your head hurts where?
My darling, did you fall with your bear?
Your mother's coming . . . shush now, here she is.
Be good now—shelved is the genius.

tr. J. H. and J. W. Prins

BIOLOGIE

O juffrouw Beekman, was u maar eencellig.
Dan kon de liefde u niet zoveel schelen.
Dan zoudt u zich gewoon in tweeën delen.
Ik geef wel toe: het is niet zo gezellig

maar heel erg praktisch. Zo'n eencellig wezen
hoeft nooit een ander wezen te aanbidden;
het deelt zich op een dag pardoes doormidden.
U kunt dat immers in de boeken lezen.

Terwijl u, met uw veertien biljoen cellen
zo treurig in de lunchroom zit te wachten.
O juffrouw Beekman, 't is al over achten.
Hij komt niet meer. Hij had toch kunnen bellen?

Hij komt niet meer. En toch, hij zei zo stellig . . .
O juffrouw Beekman, was u maar eencellig.

ZEUR NIET

Als je moe bent,
als je oud bent,
als je rillerig en miezerig en koud bent,
als je man weer met een juffrouw op de pier zit,
als de echtelijke liefde je tot hier zit,
als je schoonfamilie vraagt om ondersteuning,
als je vader zich weer vasthoudt aan de leuning,
als er sneeuw is,
als er mist is,
als het ijzelt en je minnaar een sadist is,
als dat allemaal je lot is
en je vraagt of er een god is,
sla dan woedend met de deuren,
ga je cocktail-dress verscheuren,
maar niet zeuren.

Huil in je bed,
bijt in je laken,
vloek tegen iedereen,
schreeuw van de daken,
maar zeur niet.
Trap om je heen,
wees nooit een dame

BIOLOGY

If only, Miss Beekman, you were a single cell.
Then love would not matter so much to you.
Then you could simply divide in two.
I admit: you would not like it as well

but more practical it certainly is.
A single cell is not in need of another,
but multiplies without any bother,
which the books call parthenogenesis.

But you with your cells, fourteen billion in all,
sit forlorn in the lunchroom, and wait, and wait.
Miss Beekman, now it is well past eight.
He is not coming. Why did he not call?

He is not coming. But he meant so well . . .
If only, Miss Beekman, you were a single cell.

tr. J. H. and J. W. Prins

DON'T WHINE

When you're tired,
when you're old,
when you're miserable, shivering and cold,
when your husband picks up a new girlfriend,
when matrimonial bliss leaves you bored no end,
when your in-laws are asking for money,
when your father is reeling with brandy,
when it's snowing,
when there's fog and mist,
when it's drizzling and your lover's a sadist,
when all of this turns out to be your lot,
and you wonder if there really is a god,
then throw a fit and slam the door,
rip up your cocktail dress from Dior,
but don't whine.

Cry in your bed,
chew on your sheets,
curse at everyone,
shout in the streets,
but don't whine.
Kick all around you,
never be a lady,

en gooi het theeservies
dwars door de ramen,
maar zeur niet.
Neem een grote schaar en knip in het velours,
scheld de vrouw van de notaris uit voor hoer,
doe dat allemaal,
maak een grof schandaal,
maar zeur niet.

Als je down bent,
als je ziek bent,
als je kromgetrokken van de rimmetiek bent,
als de regen door het dak lekt op de grond
en je zeven kinders hebben rooie hond
en geen stukje eten in de frigidaire
en de muizen vallen morsdood in de serre,
als je Austin op een paal botst,
als de kat weer op de mat van het portaal kotst,
als je arm bent als een kerkmuis,
moet gaan dweilen in een werkhuis,
ja, dat alles kan gebeuren,
zelfs in technicolorkleuren,
ga niet zeuren.

Spring in de gracht
of knip je haar af,
duw oude dametjes
van het trottoir af,
maar zeur niet.
Ga judo leren,
ga striptease dansen,
schiet je revolver leeg,
peng, op Pierre Janssen,
maar zeur niet.
Ga naar 't postkantoor en spuug door het loket,
krijg een hartaanval of ga desnoods naar bed
met de kardinaal,
doe dat allemaal,
maar zeur niet.

Raak aan de drank,
haat al je vrindjes,
breek in bij Luns,
pik al z'n lintjes,
maar zeur niet.

Ransel je kind,
knijp je parkietje,

pick up your tea set
and break it in two,
but don't whine.
Take giant scissors and cut up the velour,
call the notary's wife a shameless whore,
do it all,
create a scandal,
but don't whine.

When you're down,
when you're ill,
when arthritis leaves you stiff in a chill,
when rain leaks through the roof to the ground,
and your seven children all have the chickenpox,
and not a morsel is left in the icebox,
and the mice all drop dead near the breadbox,
when your Austin crashes into a tree,
when your cat throws up on the settee,
when you're as poor as a churchmouse,
have to mop floors in someone else's house,
yes, all this can happen to you,
and even in technicolor too,
but don't start whining.

Jump in the canal,
cut off your hair,
push little old ladies
down the stair,
but don't whine.
Take up karate,
dance in the nude,
take your revolver
and shoot down some dude,
but don't whine.
Visit the post office and spit at the clerk,
Have a heart attack or go berserk
seducing the cardinal,
do it all,
but don't whine.

Get rip-roaring drunk,
insult your relations,
break in at the Prime Minister's
and steal his prize decorations,
but don't whine.

Whack your kid,
pinch your parrot,

zeg tot de generaal
"u bent een mietje,"
maar zeur niet.

Doe dat allemaal,
wees een kannibaal,
maar zeur niet.

BRONTË, DICKINSON & KIE

Eating one's heart out . . . inderdaad, dit is
'n ongekend gekonsentreerde dis
waarop die een en ander Emily teer
terwyl sy rustig wegkwyn en floreer.

INSPIRASIE

Daar is IETS wat jou stowwerige woorde gryp,
rondskommel, vaspen of verstoot
tot hy sy sin kry en soetjies wegsluip.
Paai hom as jy hom nie kan ontwyk,
dink aan hom eerder as slapend dan dood.

tell the general,
"You're a faggot,"
but don't whine.

Do it all,
be a cannibal,
but don't whine.

tr. J. H. and J. W. Prins

ELISABETH EYBERS (1915)

BRONTË, DICKINSON & CO.

Eating one's heart out . . . to be sure, it is
a singularly concentrated dish
on which the various Emilies are nourished
while they serenely waste away and flourish

tr. J. H. and J. W. Prins in collaboration with the author

INSPIRATION

SOMETHING grabs hold of your dusty words,
shaking up, pinning down, shoving aside,
it slinks away softly when satisfied.
If you cannot evade it, cajole it instead,
think of it rather as sleeping than dead.

tr. by the author

SO-CALLED

The so-called artis-
tic temperament
is straight as a blade
and craftily bent
it dilates like a heart
and shuts tight like a fist
it clamps you apart
cut down to size
it puts you wise
however inane
it drives you desperate
and keeps you sane.

written in english

KREET

Selde, en steeds onverwag,
swel 'n klanklose kreet in my keel
oor alles vergaan en vergeet
wanneer die ritmiese dag
swig vir onomkeerbare nag
van absoluut niks meer weet.
Omdat menslike waardigheid
my nog altyd smoor soos 'n kleed
kan ek die dierlike kreet
nie ten gehore bring:
die geluid wat my strot binnedring
flits buite bestek van ore,
geen omstander sal dit noteer
vóór die beklinkende keer.
Tot dán geld ek bloot as gebore.

VIRGO

Zij is een wezen tussen vrouw en knaap.
Zij heeft de strakke passen van een jongen—
Soms ligt zij als een poes inééngedrongen,
dan schijnt zij vrouw en glimlacht in haar slaap.

Haar ogen zijn van amber, en die weten
veel wegen die haar mond aan geen verraadt.
Zij spiegelt zich in 't water als zij baadt,
haar lijf is rank en koel en nooit bezeten.

Zij houdt van lichte bloemen zonder geur,
lang kan zij zwemmen in de groene bronnen.—
Zij leest veel en aandachtig, zoals nonnen
dat doen, alléén, achter gesloten deur,

terwijl het zonlicht aan de wanden fluistert
en 't glas-in-lood raam donker glanst als wijn.

Zij heeft de trots van hen die eenzaam zijn,
een hart dat wacht, en aan de stilte luistert.

CRY

Rarely, and time after time
by way of utter surprise,
an inaudible cry fills my throat
because of what dwindles and dies
as soon as the rhythmic day
makes way for unbiddable night
stripped of all sound and all sight.
Whilst human dignity
still smothers me like a cloak
I can't voice the animal cry
that chokes me, no eardrum can thrill
to its quavering, however forlorn;
no onlooker takes note before
it actually strikes like a drill.
Till then I just count as being born.

tr. by the author

HELLA S. HAASSE (1918)

VIRGO

Half woman, half boy, a creature in between:
She has a young lad's brisk and sturdy gait—
but when asleep, curled softly like a cat,
she seems a woman, smiling in her dream.

Her eyes are amber and know all the best
secluded paths her tongue never betrays.
She watches her reflection as she bathes,
her body's slender, cool and unpossessed.

She likes unscented flowers, white or pale,
and lingers long when swimming in green springs.—
With books she's quiet, rapt in ponderings,
alone, the way a nun reads in her cell

while sunlight whispers on the walls and paints
a glow as dark as wine in leaded glass.

She has the pride that comes of loneliness,
a heart attuned to silence as it waits.

tr. Myra Scholz

[IK ZAG CASSANDRA IN 'T CONCERTGEBOUW]

Ik zag Cassandra in 't Concertgebouw:
een wazig scherm van strakgespannen snaren
stond tussen mij en deze donkre vrouw
stond tussen mij en haar bezeten staren
Zij ranselde een harp met smalle hand
de glazen klanken braken aan haar schouder
—een melodie uit een verloren land—
al spelende scheen zij vermoeid en ouder
en rampenzwart uitzinnig werd haar blik
Zij kreunde onder losgewoelde haren
joeg over ons een wilde golf van schrik
een visioen van opgezweepte scharen
de ijzerharde marsdreun van de tijd
en alle doden wenkten aan de wanden
't orkest bad schreeuwend naar de eeuwigheid
wij zaten in een hel van licht te branden.

[EIERSCHALEN TOT DE RAND GEVULD]

Eierschalen tot de rand gevuld
met tranen dragen wij
behoedzaam door de tijd.

In de spiegels onzer ogen
rijst de wereld onherbergzaam op.
Overal zijn wij geweest.
Nergens keren wij terug.

Beladen met herinneringen
buigen wij ons naar de aarde toe.
Onwetend en zonder wijsheid
welken wij spoorloos uit het licht.

[I SAW CASSANDRA IN THE CONCERT HALL]

I saw Cassandra in the concert hall
a screen of tense strings like a haze
stood between me and that dark woman
stood between me and her demonic gaze.
She plucked a harp with slender hand
shattering glassy notes across her shoulder
—a melody from a lost land—
while playing she seemed tired and older
and her eyes turned black with horror.
Her groans and her wild head of hair
sent waves of terror over us
a vision of millions swept away
through the endless iron march of the century
and all the dead beckoned at the wall
as the music's prayer screamed to eternity
and we sat burning in the light of hell.

tr. J. H. and J. W. Prins

HANNY MICHAELIS (1922)

[EGGSHELLS FILLED TO THE BRIM]

Eggshells filled to the brim
with tears, we carry them
carefully through time.

In the mirrors of our eyes
the world rises inhospitably.
We have been everywhere.
Nowhere do we return.

Burdened with memories
we stoop towards the earth.
Unknowing and unwise
we wither away from the light
without a trace.

tr. Marjolijn de Jager

[DE TRIOMFANTELIJKE MOEDERS]

De triomfantelijke moeders
achter hun kinderwagens
zouden van me walgen als
ze wisten hoe opgelucht
ik me voelde toen ik merkte
dat ik niet zwanger was
en geen moord hoefde te plegen
om te voorkomen dat door mijn toedoen
iemand gedwongen zou worden
zich aan het naargeestige leven
vast te klampen uit angst
om dood te gaan.

[ERGENS IN HUIS]

Ergens in huis
slaat hard een deur dicht
en even wankelt
de kleine giraffe
van vrolijk oranje plastic.
Geschenk van een 6-jarig
jongetje dat pendelend
tussen ontredderde ouders
zijn lot onbegrijpelijk
blijmoedig draagt.

[DRIE JAAR WAS IK ONGEVEER]

Drie jaar was ik ongeveer
toen ik op een najaarsavond
door het raam stond te kijken
met mijn neus voor het eerst
boven de vensterbank uit
zodat ik toen pas ontdekte
dat er een huis werd gebouwd
tegenover het onze. Met grote
beslistheid verkondigde ik:
dat halen ze 's zomers weer weg.
Mijn moeder die het ook niet helpen kon
moest erom lachen. Tegen het einde van

[THE TRIUMPHANT MOTHERS]

The triumphant mothers
behind their prams
would loathe me if
they knew how relieved
I felt when I found out
I wasn't pregnant
and didn't have to commit a murder
to prevent that because of me
someone would be forced
to cling to this dreary
life from fear
of dying.

tr. Ria Loohuizen

[SOMEWHERE IN THE HOUSE]

Somewhere in the house
a door slams shut
and a small giraffe
of bright orange plastic
totters briefly.
A present from a six-year-old
boy who, commuting
between bewildered parents,
bears his fate with
incomprehensible joy.

tr. Marjolijn de Jager

[I WAS THREE YEARS OLD OR SO]

I was three years old or so
on an evening in the fall
when I stood looking through the window,
my nose for the first time
higher than the window sill
and discovered only then
that a house was being built
across from ours. With great
assurance I announced:
this summer they will take it away.
My mother laughed,
she could not help it. At the end
of World War Two, when my parents

de tweede wereldoorlog toen mijn ouders
al waren vergast, staken de Duitsers
het huis in brand. Na de bevrijding
werd het weer opgebouwd. Het staat er
nog en ook ik droom nog herhaaldelijk
van betonnen en bakstenen gebouwen
die een veelbelovend uitzicht
drastisch te niet doen.

[JE GEZICHT ONHERKENBAAR]

Je gezicht onherkenbaar
van tederheid en tegelijk
vertrouwder dan het mijne
zoals het me iedere dag
onzeker aankijkt uit de spiegel.
Door de mist van verdampte
jaren flitst plotseling
haarscherp het oude vergezicht.
Met je armen om me heen
lijkt het of de ring
van mijn bestaan zich sluit.
Misschien heeft het wonder
me aangeraakt, misschien
ben ik gered.

ARGO

Iason voer toen van Iolkos naar Kolchis
woedend roeiend tegen loodrechte vloed,
Kastor, Pollux, Asklepios, Idmon,
hun oogbal verbrand door de bast van een ram,
op de horizon laaiende zon.
Nog wankel van branding snoerde hij stieren
het juk op de schoft, hun neusgat blies vlammen
hun hoeven van brons groeven de voren,
hij plantte er het zaad in, tanden van draken
waaruit reuzen ontstonden.

had been gassed, the Germans set
the house on fire. After the liberation
it was rebuilt. It stands there
still and I still dream repeatedly
of cement and brick buildings
changing a view that promises much
into nothing.

tr. J. H. and J. W. Prins

[YOUR FACE UNRECOGNIZABLE]

Your face unrecognizable
with tenderness and yet
more familiar than my own
as it looks at me from the mirror
uncertainly each day.
Suddenly through the mist of evaporated
years the old view flashes
crystal-clear.
With your arms around me
it seems as if the ring of
my existence closes.
Maybe a miracle
has touched me, maybe
I have been saved.

tr. Marjolijn de Jager

CHRISTINE D'HAEN (1923)

ARGO

Jason fared then from Iolcus to Colchis
furiously rowing against the vertical tide,
Castor, Pollux, Asclepius, Idmon,
their eyeballs burnt by the hide of a ram,
a blazing sun on the horizon.
Still tottering from breakers he tied the yoke
to the withers of bulls, their nostrils flame-blowing
their hooves of bronze ploughed the furrows
where he planted the seed, the teeth of dragons
from which giants arose.
But the king's daughter, the sorceress of the night

Maar de dochter des konings, de toverkol 's nachts
zalfde zijn lichaam met bijtende balsems
brouwde vergiften, verdoofde het ondier,
en schonk hem
de dichtdonzen zachte vochtige vacht
met een gouden weerschijn van bloed
het amber albasten
blank glanzend spannende vlies
vol, rond, zonder één wonde
gladde, gave, zwanger van vocht.

DERDE GRAFGEDICHT VOOR KIRA VAN KASTEEL

De prachtige vrouwen die den herfst versieren
met roestig bruin, fluweelen groen en ros,
den opgebonden donkerblonden tros
der haren en gebaren der feline dieren

roepen u weder op, uw kostbaar vuur
waarbij gij verwen roerde voor de wol,
eerst ruw en dan gewasschen zacht en vol,
gesponnen en geweven uur voor uur.

Glinstrend en mat gelijk een goudfazant
brak in uw diep mortier de regenboog,
scherp overwaakt door uw groot ernstig oog.
Dan werd uw kleederdracht een najaarsland:

gedempt gelijk de kleine jachtpatrijs,
gloeiend gelijk een trotsche vederdos.
Gij werdt getroffen met één schot in 't bosch,
somber bedekt met glas en winterijs.

anointed his body with stinging balsams
brewed poisons, deafened the monster
and gave him
the dense downy soft humid fleece
with a golden lustre of blood
the amber alabaster
fair shining tight-stretched fleece
full and round and without one wound
sleek, perfect, pregnant with dampness.

tr. Marcus Cumberlege

THE THIRD EPITAPH FOR KIRA VAN KASTEEL

The lovely women who adorn the fall
with velvet green, red, and rusty brown,
with their dark-blond tresses bound
and the movement of feline animals

conjure you up again, your precious fire
where you mixed the dyes for wool,
first rough, then washed soft and full,
spun and woven hour after hour.

Within your mortar and pestle a rainbow gleamed
like the dull sheen of a golden pheasant,
guarded by your sharp eyes, forever present.
Then your garment became an autumn scene:

glowing like plumage of great price,
subdued like the partridge's muted amber.
Struck by one shot in the woods, somber
underneath glass and winter ice.

tr. J. H. and J. W. Prins

NEGENDE GRAFGEDICHT VOOR KIRA VAN KASTEEL
como el ciervo

Gehorend hert, gehorend hoofd geheven
des herten, gekroonde kop, gekransde keel
met druiven, rozen; neergezonken neven
Diana naakt in 't woud, die honden streelt,

de kruik der beken kantelt, everzwijnen
laat naderen en den boog ontbindt.
O weidsch gewei, o wild dat overwint,
de jageres rust bij den god der wijnen.

Manhaftig hert, niet vluchtig, maar geschonken,
hermetisch en harmonisch, zonder haat;
dorstig naar waterbronnen, liefdedronken,
dat ongewond nog ongewonden laat.

Zoete verzoende jacht, ruigharig hert
uit bergen in de geurige kruiden: leven
eenmaal onvergelijkelijk gegeven—
dat ik bezit, dat u ontnomen werd.

GEBED VAN EEN HOER

Lieve Heer,
laat zakenlieden minder roken,
beter wassen,
minder koffie drinken
en vergeef de schuldenaren.

Dat boeren tandenpoetsen,
slagers plastic hoezen
om de koeielijken spannen
en minder stinken
voor zij mij bezoeken;
vergeef de schuldenaren.

THE NINTH EPITAPH FOR KIRA VAN KASTEEL
*como el ciervo**

Hornèd hart, horned upraised head
of hart, crowned head, throat wreathed
with grapes, roses; settled down next to
Diana nude in the wood, who strokes her hounds,

overturns the jug of brooks, makes swine
approach and releases her bow.
O broad antlers, O wild prey that triumphs,
the hunters repose with the god of the vine.

Manly hart, not fleeting, but offering devotion,
hermetic and harmonic, without hatred;
thirsting for spring water, drunk with love potions,
that leaves neither unsmitten nor unscathed.

Sweet appeased hunt, shaggy-haired hart
from mountains amid aromatic herbs: life
bestowed so incomparably rife—
which I possess, and from you departs.

tr. Scott Rollins

NEL NOORDZIJ (1923)

A WHORE'S PRAYER

Our Lord,
Let businessmen smoke less,
wash better,
drink less coffee
and forgive those who trespass.

Let farmers brush their teeth,
butchers wrap cow carcasses
in plastic bags
before paying me a visit
so they stink less;
forgive those who trespass.

---

* *"Como el ciervo"* is a poem from San Juan de la Cruz's "Cantico Espiritual" (16th century), a paraphrase of the Canticles. San Juan generally refers to "the loved one." Here the hart (or stag) signifies fleeting life itself. The image of the hart next to Diana, goddess of the hunt, appears in a bas-relief by Benvenuto Cellini (in the Louvre, 16th century).

En maak mij dit jaar dorpsbewoner
in de buurt van een rivier:
alleen.

En voor de rest:
maak alle mannen impotent
op éen na
en vergeef de schuldenaren,

Want ik ben zeer vermoeid
en neurastheen.

OP MIJN DERTIGSTE VERJAARDAG.

Nu is het wachten op de avond indigo,
teleurgesteld en bijna teder. Desperaat

rusten en eten mijn gemene kleine gedachten
tesamen met hun officieren—zeer begaafd—en

weten nog van niets. En allen snoepen en
verwennen zich in spitse tenten. Straks, zo

vraag ik mij dus af, als de signalen snerpen en
de aanval dringt: wie zal de overwinning tot mijn

drempel slepen, wie van mijn standvastige soldaten
en koekebakkers, noga-eters, met verkleefde tanden

zal de galverbitterde ongenietbare, mijn vijand
doen bijten in de dorre dorpels van mijn zand?

Ik heb de machtige middag overwonnen en driemaal
om mijn muren rondgesleurd en zegetekenen sieren

de trommel van mijn borst als stippen een insekt,
een schadelijke kever, mijn eenzame verdelging

vrees ik mateloos. En zo hertel ik in de naderende
nacht de wijkende kwartieren, ademloos, terwijl

mijn knechten vloeken in hun slechte slaap en
snuffelend mijn helden dromen van hun hoge, voor-

treffelijke paarden, gesneuvelde grootogigen, die
rotten onder velden onafzienbaar, vol varens en

And this year make me an inhabitant
of a village near a river:
alone.

And for the rest:
make all men impotent
but one
and forgive those who trespass,
because I am very tired
and neurasthenic.

    tr. Ria Loohuizen

FRITZI TEN HARMSEN VAN DER BEEK (1927)

ON MY THIRTIETH BIRTHDAY.

Now the waiting for the evening is indigo,
disappointed and almost tender. Desperate,

my mean small thoughts rest and dine
(very capably) with their officers and

do not yet know what is to come. And all overeat
and indulge themselves in their high tents. Later,

when the signals sound shrilly and the attack
presses, I ask myself who shall drag the victory

to my doorstep, which of my steadfast soldiers,
assorted cooks and candy-munchers with sticky teeth

shall make the gall-embittered, unpalatable
enemy bite in the dusty thresholds of my sand?

I have overcome the mighty afternoon and have
three times dragged it around my walls, and signs

of victory adorn the drum of my chest as dots
an insect or some harmful beetle; my lonely extinction

I fear boundlessly. And so I recount in the approaching
night the yielding hours, breathless, while

my servants curse in their troubled sleep and
my heroes dream snorting of their tall, large-eyed

magnificent horses, killed in battle and now
rotting below endless fields full of ferns

zomers loof. Zij God geloofd. Wees dus genadig,
vergelijk behoedzaam mijn voorbeeldige ondeugende

gedachten,—ordinair gekostumeerd en even stom als
strijdbaar—met mijn veel verwerpelijker, uiterst,

uiterst betrekkelijke luciditeit

INTERPRETATIE VAN HET UITZICHT.

Verschillende bomen in deze verdoemde tuin
stellen godzijdank nog paal en perk aan

een oude man die daar gedurig rond loopt, zonder
hoed, zwart als een krent in grauw gebak van

licht en landschap, ja een man van ziekte. Zwak
maar taai en onbeschoft. Hij draait, de afgeleefde

kreeft, in kringen om mijn vijvers, der seizoenen dolle
dolle naald deert hem, verstokter, blijkbaar niet.

En de verlegen bleke regen al weggebleven is, de doorluchtige
wind, voortvluchtig, in het geheime hout ontweken.

En heerst verwildering alom en willekeur haakt
bladerloos aan de ontdane hagen waarlangs aarzelend

zijn zachte schunnige verwoesting vaart. En niemand kan
hem keren waar hij zeverend door mijn bezeerde heesters breekt

en bevend speeksel kwijlt langs mijn beleefde kleine twijgen.
Van de vlugge lustige vogels geen hulp meer te verwachten is nu

de heilige reiger zelfs al ochtendlijk is uitgeweken achter de
geschonden horizon. Het is te hopen dat de mooie rode autobus

die alle oude mensen later af komt halen, hem nu spoedig
over rijdt naar ongenadiger terreinen, naar jachtvelden van

eeuwig asfalt, waarin overal verchroomde bakken voor zijn
rochels en de uitgekauwde stompen van zijn stinkende sigaren.

Want al mijn vijvers liggen dicht, mijn paadjes raken
zeer vertrapt, de schuwe schepselen hebben mijn struikgewas

verlaten, mijn heerlijkheid ligt braak. O keer, keer
welluidende wind, verliefde regen weer tot aan mijn

haveloze heuvelen

and summer's foliage. God be praised. Be merciful too,
compare cautiously my exemplary, impudent thoughts—

plainly costumed and as dumb as warlike—
with my much less acceptable, utterly relative

lucidity

tr. Manfred Wolf

INTERPRETATION OF THE VIEW.

Various trees in this cursed garden
still keep within bounds thank heavens

an old man who constantly walks around there,
without a hat, black as a currant in gray loaf of

light and landscape, yes a man of disease. Weak
but tough and insolent. This worn-out crab,

he circles around my ponds, the mad mad needle of the seasons
does not, apparently, affect him, inveterate.

And the bashful pale rain has already stayed away, the
illustrious wind, fugitive, dodged into the secret wood.

Degeneration reigns all around and caprice catches
leafless on the disconcerted hedges past which

hesitantly sails his soft scurvy destruction. And no one can
check him where he breaks through my damaged shrubs, slavering,

and all atremble slobbers spit along my polite little twigs.
No help can be expected anymore from the quick lusty birds now

the holy heron has taken refuge even mornings behind the
violated horizon. It is to be hoped that the nice red bus

that comes to get all old people in the end, will soon
drive him over to more merciless grounds, to hunting grounds of

eternal asphalt, with chrome bins everywhere for his
gobs and the chewed ends of his stinking cigars.

For all my ponds lie closed, my paths are
trodden down, the timid creatures have left

my thickets, my domain lies fallow. O return, return
melodious wind, amorous rain to my

ragged hills

tr. Greta Kilburn

HIJ

Je hebt niet meer zei hij dan dit
je knieholte je atlas en je draaier
je ogen oren en dat is dan samen
nog aardig wat zei hij en ik bleef zwijgen

je hebt niet meer en meer zal je niet krijgen
zei hij zijn stem van ongeduld wat vlak
koffie en brood een kind met sluike haren
hij zweeg terwijl hij bleef benoemen wat ik had

en daarin hing wat tussen zijn woorden
was heengeglipt op het nippertje
hing hoog en droog blind mank verkouden
bijna verschrompeld aan zijn tak
een levende vrouw in me die ik geloof.

Ze was het enige dat bewoog.

VOORBESCHIKKING

Een vrouw zou moeten trouwen met een boom of water,
maar zij is blijkbaar aangewezen op een man.
En welke man is aan een boom gelijk?
En welke man gelijkt het water?

Een liefkozing die als een meer doorzichtig
is en heel de huid omstroomt,
een hoofd dat haar met lover overschaduwt,
een kind dat door een tal van takken ademt,
altijd weer ontluikend in de lente
altijd vogelstemmen voor zijn blijheid.

God heeft aan de vrouw een echtgenoot gegeven
zonder golven, zonder schors of mossen
en omringt haar heimwee in dit leven
met zijn eindeloze zee en trotse bossen.

ANKIE PEYPERS (1928)

HE

All you've got, he said, is this:
your knees your knuckles and your spine
your eyes your ears and put together
that's quite a lot, he said, and I kept silent

that is all you've got, all you will ever get
he said with a flat voice slightly impatient
coffee and bread, a straight-haired child
in silence he went on naming what I had

and between his words there hung
in a last moment's escape from them
high and dry blind crippled sniffling
nearly shriveled on his tree
a living woman I believe in.

She was the only one that moved.

tr. by the author

PREDESTINATION

A woman should marry a tree or water,
but evidently she has been assigned a man.
And what man can be the like of a tree?
And what man can be like water?

A caress as transparant as a
lake, that washes over all one's skin,
a head of foliage that covers her with shade,
a child breathing through a wealth of branches,
always opening up again in spring,
always the sound of birds for its delight.

God has given woman a husband
without waves, without bark or mosses
and surrounds her longing in this life
with his endless sea and prideful forests.

tr. Wanda Boeke

MUIZEN

tussen mij en het zachte
krioelende nest muizen
dat je mijn hersens noemt
is maar een vaag verband

ik kijk graag naar dat nest
naar dat grijze bewegen
naar neezwiepende staarten
hardkralen ogen naar een bolle
volle muizin die weer jongt

ze lopen graag in me rond

niet veel meer dan dat

ik ben er niet zoals jij
zeker van dat verstand
meer is dan een nest muizen
dan zachte krioelende angst

WAARSCHUWING

hij
zal je afraden om wild te zijn
je tanden in zijn beeld te zetten
zijn gehavende verstening te bekijken
zal je afraden om iets te splijten

is bereid je beide ogen
pasklaar te maken voor zijn lenzen
knoeit geduldig aan je strottenhoofd
tot zijn woorden op je stemband staan
omdat hij alles voor je over heeft

en je mag naar zijn radio luisteren
en zijn wegen mag je bewandelen
zijn huizen bewonen; er zijn geen andere

trots zal hij naar je kijken
naar gods eigengereide kleuter
die mag gissen wat gaande is
die niets mag bewegen

MICE

between myself and the soft
squirming nest of mice
that you call my brains
there is but a vague connection

I like to look at that nest
at all that gray movement
at the nay-swishing tails
beady-hard eyes at a dumpling mouse
plump with young again

they like to run around in me

not much more than that

unlike you I'm not
sure that the seat of reason
is more than a nest of mice
more than a soft squirming fear

tr. Wanda Boeke

WARNING

he
will advise you not to be wild
or sink your teeth into his likeness
or watch his pitiful turning into stone
will advise you not to split anything

is prepared to have both your eyes
measured up for his lenses
will fiddle patiently with your larynx
until his words register in your vocal cords
because he'll do anything for you

and you're allowed to listen to his radio
and you're allowed to walk down his roads
live in his houses; there are no others

proudly he will look at you
at god's willful toddler
who's allowed to guess what's going on
who isn't allowed to move anything

tr. Wanda Boeke

BRIEF

aan meral taigun

dat er donkere zilveren vogels
in mijn leven zouden zijn wist ik niet
dat je me je harde steden de sprookjes
de giganten de slagschaduw zou brengen

je vliegt door de ruimte
van anatolië
je tuimelt woorden in me
fluistert ze en heft ze
als een lichtgewicht
zijn zwaarte

je stem je grimassen als je huilt
je woede je heft ze
de helft van mijn boeken vaag je weg
en je zegt "nazim"

op het toneel
in die kleine zaal
vliegen donkere zilveren vogels aan
je vliegt ze

SCHIPBREUK

Ik wilde me inschepen voor
een land waar ik nog niet bestond
onderweg ben ik verdronken

alleen om niet al te weerloos
aan te spoelen later
lieg ik een vlot
lieg ik een reddingsboei
lieg ik mijn hoofd boven water.

LETTER
to meral taigun*

that there would be dark silver birds
in my life I did not know
nor that you would bring me your white cities
your fairy tales and giants and broken shadows

you fly through the space
over anatolia
you tumble your words into me
you whisper them and lift them

your voice your distorted face your tears
your anger you lift them
half of my old books you sweep away
saying "nazim"[†]

on stage
in this small theater
dark silver birds fly in
you fly them

tr. by the author

ELLEN WARMOND (1930)

SHIPWRECKED

I wanted to embark for
a land in which I did not yet exist
but on the way I drowned

yet to be less defenseless
later when I wash ashore
I fabricate a raft
I fake a buoy
I make believe my head floats above the waves.

tr. Carla van Splunteren

---

* Meral Taigun is a Turkish actress who came to The Netherlands in the eighties. With her husband Vasif Öngören she founded the first Turkish theatre company in The Netherlands.

[†] "Nazim" refers to Nazim Hikmet (1902–1963), a famous, politically engaged Turkish poet who spent many years in prison.

MODERN TIMES

De eigentijdse naam van eigentijdse
voorwerpen maakt poezie nog niet moderner
een kunstmaan zonder meer
blijft een machine
en het woord kut maakt een gedicht
zo ouderwets als een wc-deur

alleen morele herbewapenaars
krijgen daar nog een kick van
maar het is een slappe klap
in een lauw bord pap—een rilling
in een bak gebluste kalk—
en zonde van de moeite

laat dat soort arme rijken
zichzelf maar amuseren

maar een veelgebruikt woord als bijvoorbeeld
zilver
schrijven op een manier
die je het veelgebruikte
zilver in je vullingen doet proeven.

HUMANISME VOOR KLEINBEHUISDEN

Je kunt niet alles doen
wat je zou willen maar
wel proberen veel te vermijden

door bijvoorbeeld niet als even
zoveel manke sleperspaarden
hinnikend te hinken naar de slachtbank
op de overbekende muziek
van de teutoonse blaaskaak

niets verandert
wat je niet zelf verandert
neem de tijd die je eigendom is
in je eigen hand en je hand
weg van je ogen

MODERN TIMES

Contemporary names for contemporary
objects don't make poetry any more modern
a satellite plain and simple
remains a machine
and the word cunt dates a poem
as much as the water closet door

only moral rearmament fans still
get a bang out of that
but it's a limp-wristed slap
in a bowl of lukewarm porridge—a shiver
in a tub of slaked lime—
and a waste of energy

let those poor rich
have their fun

but writing a well-worn word like
silver
for instance in a way
that makes you taste
the well-worn silver in your fillings.

tr. Maria Jacobs

HUMANISM FOR THOSE WHO LIVE IN CRAMPED QUARTERS

You can't do everything
you want to but
you can try to avoid a lot

by for instance not limping
like so many workhorses
to the slaughterhouse
whinnying to the over-familiar sounds
of teutonic windbags

nothing changes
that you don't change yourself
take the time that is your property
in your own hands and take your hands
away from your eyes

men kan denken: nee
en kan denken:
het helpt je geen donder maar toch
kan denken: nee.

IN ANTWOORD OP UW SCHRIJVEN

Een inzending voor een jaarboek?

ik weet wel wat leukers vandaag:

in de zon zitten dit bedrijven
of dat
of andere unprintables
waarover bezorgde leraren
VHMO
later schrijven zullen: "het toppunt
van obsceniteit voor een vrouw,
(en dan nog in het engels bovendien!)"

en ik me maar afvragen wat
het toppunt van obsceen
dan voor een mán wel zijn zal

misschien wel de moral standard
van een leraar VHMO.

OP ZOEK NAAR GERTRUDE STEIN

Een kamer zwaar van overjarig zwijgen,
Mesdames, Messieurs,
rue de Fleurus . . .
Zij stierf in vijfenveertig, nadat Yanks
haar gasten waren, potente bevrijders,
verlegen lotgenoten en zwaarstandige fantasten.
De kamer was vol geur van oude dames,
Gertrude en Alice,
en vol herinnering aan jonge dames,
Alice, en de bevriende Amazones.
1910, 1914, 1918 . . .

you can think: no
and can think:
it doesn't do a damn bit of good but still
can think: no.

tr. Manfred Wolf

IN REPLY TO YOUR LETTER

A contribution to a yearbook?

I know something more amusing for today:

sitting in the sun, committing this
or that
or other unprintable
about which worried high-school teachers
will say later: "the ultimate
in obscenity for a woman
(and she wrote it in English!)"

and I asking myself what
the ultimate obscenity
for a man would be . . .

perhaps the moral standard
of a high-school teacher.

tr. Manfred Wolf

ANDREAS BURNIER (1931)

LOOKING FOR GERTRUDE STEIN

A room heavy with the silence of too many years.
Mesdames, Messieurs,
rue de Fleurus . . .
She died in forty-five, after Yankees
had been her guests, powerful liberators,
shy fellow-sufferers, heavy-headed dreamers.
The room smelled of old ladies,
Gertrude and Alice,
and the memory of young ones,
Alice, and the Amazons they befriended.
1910, 1914, 1918 . . .

Hun gezin vol Picasso en orde,
daar heerste Gertrude als een goede joodse vader,
een patriarch, streng maar beminnelijk.
Veel veiligheid op de bank,
veilig veeleisend,
veilig zich beperkend tot de omgang met mannen
met wie zij converseerde,
terwijl Alice
iedereen bediende en de dames onderhield.
Borduurwerk, thee, tapijten, Juan Gris,
Picasso, Braque, Matisse, Apollinaire.
Picasso kon niet scheiden zonder geld,
het Grand Palais was toen nog Grand Palais.
Borduurwerk, thee, tapijten, Jean Cocteau,
een wereld vol mensen.
Zij geloofde niet in de hemel voor joden:
"Wij leven alleen maar nu."

Gertrude,
als ik je tegenkom in de hemel der gojim,
Gertrude, Caesar van de eeuwwenteling,
en je begroet, dan zijn wij dus verdwaald.
Zoals jij, Caesar, verdwaalde in een vrouwenlijf,
dat je waardig naar je hand wist te zetten,
zo zul je je in de hemel ook wel redden.
Dag Gertrude,
je huis is nog mooi,
goed in de verf zoals het jou past.
Voor het Grand Palais staan ze te queuën om Picasso.
Ik weet niet of Alice nog leeft.
Dag Gertrude
binnenkort.

NOSTALGIE

onhoorbaar tussen
vallend sneeuw
roepen oude draden
de weg terug

Picasso and order prevailed in their house,
where Gertrude ruled as a good Jewish father,
a patriarch, stern but lovable.
All safe at the bank,
safely demanding all,
safely conversing
only with a few men,
while Alice
served and entertained the ladies.
Embroidery and tea, tapestry and Juan Gris,
Picasso, Braque, Matisse, Apollinaire.
Without money, no divorce for Picasso,
back then the Grand Palais was still the Grand Palais.
Embroidery and tea, tapestry and Jean Cocteau,
a world full of people.
She did not believe in a heaven for Jews:
"We only live now."

Gertrude,
if I meet you in the heaven of the Goyim,
Gertrude, Caesar of the turning century,
and greet you, then we have lost our way.
You were lost, Caesar, in a woman's body
but you knew to make the best of it,
and you will in heaven too.
So long Gertrude,
your house is still grand,
well painted as befits you.
At the Grand Palais people wait in line for Picasso.
I wonder if Alice is still alive.
So long Gertrude,
so long.

tr. J. H. and J. W. Prins

LOES NOBEL (1931)

NOSTALGIA

inaudible in
falling snow
old threads call
the road back

de evenaar spoelt ze weer
in mijn handen

gelouterd door de oceaan
vlecht ik nieuwe
meridianen

dwars door mijn kinderen heen

[HET ZIJN DE ZWARTE SCHIMMEN]

het zijn de zwarte
schimmen die mij parten spelen

tussen nog laag
groene rijsthalmen
voeten opgelost in
sawahmodder stond ik
toen de eeuwen
vloeibaar raakten
en stemmen van
vulkaan en akkerland
eenvormig in mij
binnen stroomden

[EN NA DE INDALING]

en na de indaling
dieper in mij
je voorbij gaan
aan mij
drijfnat
van dat voedende water

en dan de weemoed
van je laten gaan
ondanks de navelstreng
die eeuwen verbindt

tijden vallen weg
en tussen jou en mij
is er geen nu
geen later

the equator washes them
into my hands again

chastened by the ocean
I weave
new meridians

through my children

tr. Sheila Gogol and Erica Eijsker

[IT IS THE BLACK GHOSTS]

it is the black
ghosts that get to me

among rice stalks still
low and green
feet dissolved in
paddy mud I stood
when centuries
turned liquid
and voices of
lowland and volcano
flowed into me
as one

tr. Sheila Gogol and Erica Eijsker

[AND AFTER YOUR DESCENT]

and after your descent
deeper into me
your passing
me by
drenched
in waters that nourish

and then the sad pains
of letting you go
despite the umbilical cord
linking epochs

time falls away
and between you and me
there is no now
no later

tr. Sheila Gogol and Erica Eijsker

BAD ZWISCHENAHN, 1964

De bruid strompelt de kerk uit op te hoge hakken
en lacht haar schrijnend lachje vanonder topzwaar kapsel
en laat zich kussen door de ooms, en blijft
tussen de graven staan, en kijkt haar kleine nieuwe man nu aan.

Begonia's barsten in bloei, klimop begroeit
de middeleeuwse gevel, alles terwille van de fotograaf.
De dominee kan gaan. Nu kan hij ons
het oude altaarstuk verklaren.
De man die Jesus slaat moet blijven dwalen
hij is het joodse volk, de eeuwig wandelende jood,
het laatst werd hij gezien zegt de legende, in Bremen, 1510.

Ik slik en vraag hem in dit warm en drukkend Duitsland
Waarom zijn kerk de helden van de eerste oorlog wél
die van de tweede niet met een plaquette eert?
Zijn antwoord geldt hem, mij, god, de fotograaf, de doden:
het valt ons allemaal niet makkelijk meer
ons met onszelf te vereenzelvigen, en door te leven.

MINNAARS MINNAARS

Vreselijker wreedheid dan door vijanden begaan
wordt minnaars minnaars aangedaan.
Hoe het hoofd te bieden aan wie in dat hoofd
al binnendrong en rooft? Vijand
komt niet zo diep, bonkt tegen buitenkant.

DE ZEEMAN

Mijn vrouw, die met haar armen hoog,
haar benen wijd, rok over rok en juichend
op het uiteinde van de pier zou moeten staan!

Door al het wachten is het juichen haar vergaan,
droog zit ze op haar strozak straks, droog
kijkt ze me aan.

JUDITH HERZBERG (1934)

BAD ZWISCHENAHN, 1964

The bride hobbles out of church on too high heels
and smiles her chafed smile under topheavy hair
and lets herself be kissed by the uncles and stands
between the graves and looks her small new husband in the eyes.

Begonias burst into bloom, ivy grows
up the medieval churchfront,
all for the sake of the photographer.
Now the pastor can explain
the old altar-piece to us.
The man beating Jesus must keep roaming,
he is the Jewish people, the wandering Jew,
last seen, according to legend, in Bremen, 1510.

I swallow and ask him in this warm and stifling Germany
why his church honors the heroes of the First War
not those of the Second with a plaque.
He speaks for himself, me, god, the photographer, the dead:
It doesn't come easy for any of us
to fit into ourselves and go on.

tr. Shirley Kaufman

LOVERS LOVERS

A more ruinous cruelty than enemies suffer
is suffered, lovers on lovers.
How to hold your head up to one who already sneaked
into that head and is stealing? So deep inside
no enemy gets, thumps against the outside.

tr. Wanda Boeke

THE SAILOR

My wife should be standing, arms held high,
legs akimbo, skirt over skirt
at the very end of the pier, rejoicing!

With all the waiting, her joy has left her,
dryly she will soon sit on her straw tick, dryly
she will look at me.

Soms duurt het dagen voor ze op wil staan.
Ik geef haar eten, drinken, zoete vijgen
mijn eigen hevigheden houd ik in.

Dan komt het wonderbaarlijk smelten
dan gaat zij weer bewegen—lente!—
rennen, vult zij de emmers.

O Heilige Maria, juist is zij zacht, juist
rusten wij, armen en benen om elkaar
vaar ik weer uit.

AFWASMACHINE
aan mijn bestek

Adieu messen en vorken, ik was jullie nooit meer af.
Het is uit tussen ons. Geen toegewijd leuteren meer
tussen zachte doeken, ik stop jullie als lastige kindertjes
in een crèche, ik ben blij dat ik jullie heb,
o, ik zou jullie niet willen missen! maar nooit
meer zullen jullie als bekenden door mijn handen gaan.
Handenbindertjes! voortaan zijn jullie vaat.
Hoor eens, we moeten redelijk zijn, het gaat niet aan
die conversaties na het ontbijt, hoe was de pap,
maakte het ei erg vlekkerig, is er niet al te hard
op je gebeten en was de rabarber verfrissend?

En het douwderideine lepeltje mijn deukje mijn
klein fijn mongooltje, moet jij ook door de molen?

O grote opscheplepel worden je kinderen nu voortaan
zonder aanzien des persoons door het water geslagen?

Wij moeten niet kinderachtig zijn. Warme sopjes
hebben hun tijd gehad. De wereld eist ons op
voor gewichtiger zaken. Mijn persoonlijkheid
bijvoorbeeld, moet nog ontplooid. Dat
kan natuurlijk niet met jullie, of met de kopjes.

Sometimes it's days before she'll get up.
I give her food, drink, sweet figs
my own exuberances I hold in check.

Then comes that wondrous melting
she starts to move again—springtime!—
to run, she fills the buckets.

Oh Holy Maria, now she is soft, now
we are resting, arms and legs entwined
I sail away again.

tr. Wanda Boeke

THE DISHWASHER
to my cutlery

Farewell knives and forks, I'll never wash you again.
This is the end of our affair. No more fond chitchat
between soft linen. I'll bundle you into a crèche like
troublesome children. I'm glad to have had you, couldn't
bear to part with you, but your familiar features
won't pass through my hands again.
My little charges; as of now you're just dirty dishes.
Listen, let's be reasonable. They just won't do,
these conversations after breakfast: was the porridge
all right, did the egg leave stains, did they bite too
hard on you and was the rhubarb refreshing?

And my rickety-rackety lopsided baby, my
sweet tiny spoon, must you be rinsed with the rest?

Ah, noble soup ladle, will your offspring henceforth
be rudely drenched without regard to rank?

Let's not kid ourselves. Of course you understand
the age of putting things to soak is past.
Our days are filled with weightier affairs.
Personalities in need of development, like mine,
just don't have time to wash by hand.

tr. John Rudge

TIJD

mijn moeder telde veel.
haar leven gemeten in data
het jaar heringedeeld:
een nieuwe vreemde kalender
van de dag waarop Opa
en de dag waarop Judith
naar de dag waarop Ronnie
en zo verder
tot de alle twaalf weer jarig
weggehaald en verdwenen waren

op school was ik angstig bij rekenen:
welk verdriet werd er in sommen gemeten?

mijn moeder heeft haar les geleerd,
bijna alles verloren, ook de laatste kat dood
telt ze de rozen en de viooltjes in haar tuin.
haar zal het leven niet meer overvallen
niemand zal meer weggaan behalve zijzelf

ik schrijf woorden
en leer mijzelf opnieuw rekenen:
na de toch nog voltooide rouw
de eerlijk verdiende eigen tijd
om wie weet gewoon verder te mogen leven

DE LAATSTE TREDE

ter herinnering aan mijn tante Judith Waagenaar, geboren
11 mei 1906, vergast in Auschwitz 3 december 1942

er werd gebeld: ik trek voorgoed aan het touw
wie is daar? roept mijn kinderstem
en staar de trap omlaag
waar jij beneden, struikelend, in haast
dezelfde tree opnieuw begint
op weg naar mij je naam
en nooit vergeten tederheden roepend

SONJA POS (1936)

TIME

My mother used to count a lot:
her life marked off by dates
a rearrangement of the year:
a new strange calendar
from the day when Grandpa
and the day when Judith
to the day when Ronnie
and so on
till all twelve had had their birthdays
and had been taken away to vanish

at school arithmetic frightened me:
what sorrow was measured in sums?

my mother learned her lesson well,
almost everything lost, even the last cat dead
she counts the roses and the violets in her garden.
life can spring no more surprises
no one will go away but she

I write words
and having reached at last against all odds
the end of mourning, I teach myself
arithmetic anew:
the well-deserved time of my own
given to me to live, who knows,
a normal life like anyone.

      tr. Ankie Peypers and Sonja Pos

THE BOTTOM STEP

**In memory of my aunt Judith Waagenaar, born the 11th of
May 1906, killed in Auschwitz the 3rd of December 1942**

The bell rang: I press the button
to open the door for good.
"Who is it?" calls the voice of the child I was
and I peer down the stairs
where you, stumbling below in haste,
try that same step again and again
on your way to me calling your name
and tender words never forgotten

ik groei en wacht op het uniek moment
dat uit het duister je gezicht
weer op zal stijgen in het licht
en mij eens de omhelzing wordt geschonken
met wie als enige mij zeker had herkend

maar gescheiden door voltooide tijd
kan ik niet dalen tot de laatste bocht
om wie ik als geen ander zocht
weer in het licht te halen
en jou en mij te redden van verlorenheid

raak ik ooit van jouw dood bevrijd?
aan turen in donkerte ontstegen?
je bent gestorven halverwege
maar blijft—steeds meer mijn kind—
om troost op weg naar mij.

[DE RIBBEN VAN DE BRUG LIGGEN]

De ribben van de brug liggen
Als wervels in de lymfe van
De lucht en trillen van hitte.
Rug, die zich spant van de oever
Naar een overkant. Door het land-
Schap flitsen spiegels, ruiten,
Blinkende lemmetten. Wind
Rolt op licht gedragen over de
Golven aan, zijn slaven. Stralend
Zijn ze gebogen onder zijn

Koninklijke slagen. De hemel
Gorgelt kort uit haar metalen
Kelen. Achter hun namen rusten
Onzichtbaar dorpen en steden.
Wildernis van verbindingen,
Strekking van ribben; ik glijd
Langs de knopen van haar rug,

I grow, waiting for the unique moment
when from the dark your face will rise
once more into the light
and I'll receive the gift of the embrace
with the only one who would not fail to see me

but set apart by time gone by
I can't descend the stairs to where
they wind that one last time
to lift again into the light
the one and only I tried to find
to save both you and me from oblivion and loss.

will I ever be free of your death?
released from peering into darkness?
you died half way
but—more and more my child—you'll always be
on your way to me for comfort.

tr. Ankie Peypers, Sonja Pos, and Wanda Boeke

ELLY DE WAARD (1940)

[THE RIBS OF THE BRIDGE ARE LAID OUT]

The ribs of the bridge are laid out
Like vertebrae in the lymph of
The air and tremble in the heat.
Back that arches from the bank
To an other side. Through the land-
Scape flash mirrors, windowpanes,
Glinting edges of blades. Wind
Rolls in carried on light over the
Crests of waves, his slaves. Blazing
They run stooped beneath his

Royal blows. The sky briefly
Gurgles out of her metallic
Throats. Villages, cities reside
Invisibly behind their names.
Wilderness of interconnections,
An extension of ribs; I slide
Down the nodes of her back,

Touwladder naar een jungle van
Geluk. Tussen de wegen en het
Doel, is daar een juiste midden?

[OP ZILVEREN VOETEN TRIPPELT]

Op zilveren voeten trippelt
Het bestek door het gerecht. Zij
Zit kaarsrecht, ik zit gebogen.
Statig als zeppelins drijven
Insekten tussen de rozen
Die met hun knoppen de contouren
Van Istanboel opvoeren, maar
Zonder minaretten. Ik diste
Ons geluk op maar mijn honger
Naar haar lust geen voedsel dan van

Haar aard. Koelte wuiven wij ons
Toe met de servetten. Ik wil haar
Naakter, haar rug die glad is als
Ivoor dat door de beduimeling van
Duizend en één nacht ingesleten
Is wil ik vervolmaakt zien. Lak
Spat van haar nagels als haar
Gehakte lopen om de tafel
Nadert. Ik leg haar in het gras en
Vouw haar als een waaier open.

[WIE KAN PLATO'S SYMPOSION NOG]

Wie kan Plato's Symposion nog
Lezen, waar vrouwen voor het gesprek
Worden weggestuurd en als hoogste
Liefde die tussen mannen wordt
Aangeprezen? Welke vrouw met
Zelfrespect? Alles moet opnieuw
Geschreven! Mijn vriend, die zijn
Manchetten met paperclipsen knoopt,
Het liefst die van zijn rok, hem wees
Ik erop dat de hoogst georganiseerde

Rope ladder toward a jungle of
Bliss. Between the back roads and the
End, is there a true mean?

       tr. Wanda Boeke

[ON SILVER FEET THE CUTLERY]

On silver feet the cutlery
Tiptoes through the main course. She sits
Straight as a board while I slouch.
Stately as zeppelins insects
Hover among the roses
Whose buds enact the contours
Of Istanbul, but without the
Minarets. I dished up our
Happiness, but my appetite
For her has no taste for a food

Other than hers. We fan ourselves
With the napkins. I want her
Barer; her back as smooth as
Ivory worn by the fingering
Of a thousand and one nights
I want to see wholly perfect. Polish
Spatters off her nails as her high-
Heeled movement around the table
Nears. I lay her out in the grass and
Open her like a fan unfolding.

       tr. Wanda Boeke

[WHO CAN READ PLATO'S SYMPOSIUM]

Who can read Plato's Symposium
Anymore, where even before the
Discussion begins the women are
Sent away, where the highest lauded
Love is that between men? What self-
Respecting woman? It will all
Have to be rewritten! To my friend,
Who buttons his cuffs with paper clips,
Preferably the ones from his tux, I
Pointed out that the most highly

Samenlevingen van dieren de
Gefeminiseerde zijn en hij
Schrok. Maar ons discours—over de
Wrok—was luchtig en geleerd en wij
Dineerden. Spoedig zag men ons op
De dansvloer, in een foxtrot, hij
Volgde en ik leidde. O het was
Een plezier, alles moest op zijn
Kop en ook zo blijven, daar
Stonden wij inmiddels op.

ANADYOMENE

Zo mooi, zoals haar naakte
Lichaam door de branding springt,
De borsten hoog, de armen
In het verlengde van haar rug
Geheven. Ik zie onder haar
Huid als nooit ontwikkelde
Vleugels die zich willen uit-
Slaan haar schouderbladen zich
Driftig bewegen. Een on-
Verminkte Venus is zij,

Levend uit het gemarmerd
Schuim herrezen. Ah, lieflijk
Zoals haar zachtheid de
Gespierde golven weerstaat! Haar
Handen houdt ze voor de holten
Met het stugge haar. Voor haar
Knielen de rotsen, rustend
Tegen elkaar en bieden ze
De door een meester geslepen
Vormen van hun ruggen

Aan. Voor hun sculptuur had
De polijster van het getij zijn
Eeuwen nodig, maar de natuur
Heeft haar volmaakt gemaakt
In nog geen eenendertig jaar.

Developed animal societies
Are the feminized ones, and he
Was stunned. But our discourse—about
Resentment—was light and learned and we
Dined. Soon we were to be seen on
The dance floor, doing a foxtrot.
He followed and I led. Oh what
A joy, it all had to be turned
On its head and stay that way, on that
We had meanwhile agreed.

tr. Wanda Boeke

ANADYOMENE

So beautiful, the way her
Naked body leaps through the
Breakers, her breasts high, her arms
An extension of her back
Reach up. Beneath her skin like
Still never developed
Wings that want to open
Out, I see her shoulder blades
Moving briskly. An un-
Disfigured Venus she is,

Rising from the marbled
Foam, alive. Ah, how sweet
The way her softness
Withstands the muscled waves! She
Holds her hands in front of the
Hollows with wiry hair. Rocks
Kneel down before her, resting
Against each other offering
The masterfully polished
Forms of their backs to

Her. In sculpting their masses
The polisher of the tides needed his
Eons, but nature was able
To create her perfection
In a brief thirty-one years.

tr. Wanda Boeke

[DE BERGEN ROKEN VAN DE HERFST-VUREN]

De bergen roken van de herfst-
Vuren die ze stoken, de bomen
Krijgen rode wangen van hun
Gloed. Ik trok naar het Noorden door
De donkerende wouden van
Europa, roestend van najaar,
Roestig van auto's, door dorpen
Zonder trottoir, als kloven, de
Lange schaduw van oktober
Woont er al. Langs zenuwbanen

Die door de valleien lopen—
In grijs van treinen en van
Wegen en alles nat van regen—
Pulseert de metalen golfstroom
Van het verkeer. Het Westen is
Eenzaam nu het millennium
Zijn einde vindt. Wat de wolken,
Het rag van industrieën, weg-
Vaagt en van de akkers aanblaast
Is een vrouwelijke wind.

PINKSTERMORGEN

heel even zoals vroeger
wee van het lange waken
loom bijeenliggen terwijl de veer
van het verlangen weer
langzaam begint te spannen,
doornat, moe van geluk

vogels schreeuwen door elkaar ergens
krankzinnig
hun buigzame stemmen raken verstrengeld
kronkelen en bloeien zoals een
teer smeedijzeren hekwerk

o, hoe eerbiedig rust ik nu en adem
in de barokke ochtend

[THE MOUNTAINS SMOKE FROM THE AUTUMN-FIRES]

The mountains smoke from the autumn-
Fires they stoke, and all the trees
Have ruby cheeks from the
Glow. I was going to the North
Through the darkening forests of
Europe, rusting in the autumn,
Rusty with cars, through villages
Without sidewalks, like chasms, the
Long shadow of October
Already dwells there. Along neural

Pathways that pass through the valleys—
In the gray of highways and of
Trains and everything's wet with rain—
The metallic gulf stream
Of the traffic pulsates. The West is
Lonely now, the millennium
Is ending. What is sweeping away
The clouds, the web of industry,
And blowing in from the fields
Is a womanly wind.

tr. Wanda Boeke

ERIKA DEDINSZKY (1942)

PENTECOST MORNING

just briefly as we used to
lie together languidly
faint from long hours waking
while the spring
of desire slowly
becomes taut again,
soaked through, tired with bliss

somewhere birds are screaming all at once
insane
their flexible voices entwining
coiling and flowering like
tenderly wrought ironwork

oh, how reverently I rest and breathe
in this bejeweled morning

het gordijn wijkt, een vrouwenrok, voor jou
bollend in de wind of misschien, voor mij
jong groen schaamhaar van opgewonden bomen
het zwelt, rijst, bloed klopt in zijn plooien
nu valt het en beeft krachteloos
eindelijk spuiten de eerste stralen van licht

we zijn pasgeboren vochtig en broos

ik zwijg met jouw zwijgen
jij slaapt met mijn gezicht

UIT DE CYCLUS "EEN VROUW BEZOEKEN"

IV

Kapok. Het opklapbed. Verloren tijd?
IJsbloemen staan te dringen voor de ruiten.
Jasmijnthee en een legertje beschuiten
voeren op tafel een vergeefse strijd
aantrekkelijk te schijnen als ontbijt.
Wanneer ze kokhalst neemt ze twee besluiten:
ze gaat zich niet aan eten meer te buiten
en blijft verwachten dat hij haar bevrijdt.

Hij heeft de honden om de tuin geleid.
Gewillig laten deuren zich ontsluiten.
In nevels van kapok kleedt hij zich uit en
liefkoost het touw dat in haar dijen snijdt.

V

Diep in de put waar haar gebeente ligt,
verschijnt hij elke avond als haar slaaf
en maakt haar uit elkaar gevallen lichaam gaaf
en brengt weer trekken aan op haar gezicht.

Wanneer zij op haar voetstuk zich verheft,
kracht, aan zijn spijt ontleend, haar schouders schraagt
en hij—van schuld vervulde dwerg—vergeving vraagt
voor wat zijn hand haar aangedaan heeft, treft

the curtain yields, a woman's skirt, for you
billowing in the wind or perhaps for me
young green pubescent fuzz of trees aroused,
it swells, rises, blood pulses in its folds
then falls and feebly trembles—
at last the first streams of light spray forth

we are newly born moist and frail

I keep silent with your silence
you are sleeping with my features

tr. Marjolijn de Jager

NEELTJE MARIA MIN (1944)

FROM THE CYCLE "TO VISIT A WOMAN"

IV

Kapok. The hideaway bed. Just wasted time?
Flowers of frost crowd around the windows.
The jasmine tea and ranks of crispy toast
upon the table unsuccessfully vie
to be a breakfast tempting to the eye.
Two things she determines as she chokes:
she won't let her appetite get out of control,
and expects that he will free her by and by.

He has led the dogs down garden paths.
Doors let themselves so easily be opened.
In fogbanks of kapok he removes his clothes and
caresses the rope that's cutting into her thighs.

V

Deep in the pit that holds her skeleton,
he materializes as her slave each night
and sets her disintegrated body right
and puts expression on her face again.

When on her pedestal she stands erect,
lent strength by his remorse her shoulders harden,
and he—guilt-filled midget—asks her pardon
for what his hand has done to her, he gets

hem van haar stalen mond het snijdend spreken.
Hij voelt van zijn geduld de vliezen breken
en steekt zijn mes ver in haar trotse rug.

Een held is hij. Hij heeft het kwaad bestreden.
Hij legt devoot en met zichzelf tevreden
het zware deksel op de put terug.

VII

Een jurk met stroken van satijn
beslaat van hoofd- tot voeteneind
als een geknotte fee het bed.
Gesluierd staat een stoel erbij.

Aan haar lijkt alles porselein.
Het pas gewreven voorhoofd glimt.
Een kleine rimpel schiet voorbij.
Diep in haar keel begint gegons
van lachen dat niet verder komt.

Haar handen spelen met haar vlecht.
Ze strikt het lint er telkens om.
Ze denkt, maar heeft nog niets gezegd.

Waar wacht hij op?

Zijn vraag verpulvert in de lucht.
Haar aandacht die naar verten vlucht
verraadt het antwoord dat hij ducht.

De kamer tolt. In haar gezicht
maakt bangheid plaats voor ongeloof
als hij het wapen op haar richt.

Na het gedempte schot slaat schrik
zijn woede stuk en onverhoopt
stelt hem haar aanblik schadeloos.
Haar stille schoonheid biedt hem troost.

Zo: in haar witte ondergoed,
als rozen aan het hart geklemd
geronnen bloed waarop haar hand
ligt uitgespreid,
is zij toch ook zijn bruid.

from her cold mouth of steel its cutting words.
He feels the tissues of his patience burst
and deep in her proud back he plants his knife.

He is a hero, has battled evil's curse.
Devotedly he puts the heavy cover
back on the pit and is well satisfied.

VII

A dress trimmed with bands of satin
takes up the bed from head to foot,
like an amputated fairy.
Veiled, a chair stands to the side.

She seems to be all porcelain.
Freshly scrubbed her forehead shines.
A tiny wrinkle flits across.
Deep in her throat the low-pitched murmur
of a laugh that goes no further.

Her hands toy idly with her braid.
She reties the ribbon over and over.
She's thinking, but hasn't yet replied.

What's he waiting for?

His question crumbles in the air.
Her thoughts fleeing far from there
betray the answer he can't bear.

The room starts reeling. On her face
the fear makes way for disbelief
as he points the gun at her and aims.

After the dull blast the shock
shatters his rage, to his surprise
the sight of her is compensation.
Her quiet beauty comforts him.

Even like this: in her white underclothes,
like roses pressed against her heart
the clotted blood on which her hand
lies, fingers spread,
she is still his bride.

VIII

Haar schaduw was mijn onderdak.
Een kamer zonder deur en zonder ramen,
waar ik alleen gelaten met mijn schaamte
om wat ik wist dat binnenin mij stak:
een horig wezen dat serviel en zwak
zichzelf verfoeide—over haar gedaante
met onvoorwaardelijke eerbied sprak.

Zij sloeg en schreef mij tranen voor
en ik betaalde maar.
Wat waarde had werd schade toegebracht.
Hoe schamel was wat overbleef
na zoveel jaar.

Nu ben ik dood voor haar.
Een naamloos lichaam dat met graagte
wordt afgeknaagd tot het geraamte blijft.

IX

De kamer is er een op schaal
nu zij ineengedoken zit
bedolven onder zijn verhaal.

Hij schalt van vloer tot zoldering,
van glazen wand tot glazen wand
verbeten zijn beschuldiging.

Zijn stem is als het weer zo koud.
Op knieën bij de kachel draalt
het meisje met het aanmaakhout.

Het durft niet op te kijken bij
bekende woorden en het bidt
o houd de liefde ver van mij.

Sneeuw waait naar binnen. Neemt bezit
van wie er is. Vereeuwigd zijn
man, vrouw en meisje in het wit.

VIII

Shelter her shadow was for me.
A room with neither door nor windowpane,
where I was alone, abandoned to my shame
over what I knew was stuck inside of me:
a serf-like being, servile and weak,
that loathed itself—that spoke of her traits
with unconditional esteem.

She beat me and sentenced me to tears
and I just kept on paying.
Anything of value suffered damage.
How paltry what was left
after so many years.

Now I'm dead to her.
A nameless body that is glad
to be gnawed away until it's bone.

IX

The room is one that's back to scale
now she is sitting huddled up
inundated by his tale.

He trumpets clear from floor to ceiling,
from wall of glass to wall of glass
his accusation seething.

Like the weather his voice is cold.
The girl dawdles with the kindling,
upon her knees before the stove.

She doesn't dare look up when she hears
familiar words, but prays in quiet
O, don't ever let love come near.

Snow blows in. Of all inside
it takes possession. Eternally here
are man, woman, and girl in white.

tr. Wanda Boeke

TOEN IK OPKEEK

Toen ik opkeek,
een gezicht zag,
onbekend,
woorden niet herkende,

was het plotseling niet meer
dan het kneden
van een lichaam
dat alleen als lijf
bekendheid had.

Je zwoegde, hoofd rood,
zweetdruppel op schouderblad,
en mond half open

en ik verteerde langzaam
tot een eenzaam vergrijp.

CONVERSATIE MET DE KINDEREN

Aan tafel gaat het over
wreed. Dat je een lied zingt
waar de ander van moet huilen,
en dat je dat wéét, zeggen zij
zwaaiend met hun lepels. Zeker.

Of met een licht de trage
zwarte kreeften lokt. Jij
in de boot. De dieren spoeden
zich, kunnen niet anders doen
dan ijlen naar wat trillend
fonkelt achter raster dood.

CHRISTA EELMAN (UNKNOWN)

WHEN I LOOKED UP

When I looked up,
saw a face
I did not know,
words I did not recognize,

it suddenly was no more
than the kneading
of a body
that was known
as flesh alone.

You were toiling, head flushed,
drops of sweat on shoulder blade,
and mouth half open

and I slowly decomposing
into lonely outrage.

tr. Marjolijn de Jager

ANNA ENQUIST (1945)

CONVERSATION WITH THE KIDS

At the table it's all about
cruelty. That you sing a song
that makes another person cry,
and that you *know* it, they say
waving their spoons. Sure.

Or with a light attract
the slow black lobsters. You
in the boat. The creatures hurry
along, can do nothing else
but scurry to what quivers
sparkling behind a grid of death.

Het ergste is de dolkstoot,
vinden zij. Dat iets geheels en
gaafs zo onverhoeds wordt aan-
getast en voortaan niet meer zelf is
maar in binding met het wapen
dat zich toegang eist, en breekt, en krast.

Ontroerd, geobsedeerd, verwond
hoor ik hoe zij het wapentuig
van liefde argeloos als wreed
benoemen. Zonder aarzeling.
Boven de soep houd ik mijn mond.

(Schumann, *Kinderszenen*, opus 15)

VANUIT DE KEUKEN
Voor L.

Mijn zilverharige vriendin en ik
zijn als twee grote appelbomen
steviger en heerlijker dan ooit in bloei,
voor de bongerd gerooid wordt.

Wanneer wij elkaar spreken, bijvoorbeeld
over het best-bewaarde damesgeheim
aller tijden, of over hoe wij ons
voegen naar de wet van de wereld,

almaar, en waarom, zegt zij mij:
wij zijn bang voor onze eigen kracht.
En inderdaad, met vreugdevolle
en opbolderende angst zeil ik daarna

de trap af: welke onderneming zal ik
nu eens gaan oprichten, welke harde
waarheid beschrijven; en ga ik, immers
in vlam, die oorlog eens voeren?

The worst is the stab of the knife,
they believe. That something whole and
sound so unexpectedly gets at-
tacked and hence is not itself anymore
but bonded with the weapon
that forces its way, and breaks, and scrapes.

Moved, obsessed, wounded,
I listen to how they blithely
label love's weaponry
as cruel. Without a second thought.
Over my soup I keep my mouth shut.

(Schumann, *Kinderszenen,* opus 15)
   tr. Wanda Boeke

FROM THE KITCHEN
   For L.

My silver-haired friend and I
are like two large apple trees
blooming more firmly and deliciously than ever,
before the orchard is to be cleared.

Whenever we talk, for instance
about the best-kept ladies' secret
ever, or discuss the way we
conform to the law of the world,

all the time, and why, she tells me:
we are afraid of our own strength.
And sure enough, with joyful
and ebullient fear I then sail

down the stairs: what endeavor shall I
go and undertake, which hard
truth describe; and am I, now all
afire, ever going to wage that war?
   tr. Wanda Boeke

[WEND NIET HET GEZICHT AF—MIJN MOEDER]

wend niet het gezicht af—mijn moeder
ook ik ben stukgewaaid maar
afstand krimpt en er is geen ruimte zonder jou

wereldzeeën zijn bevaren
kronkelpaden bezocht—helaas
mijn vergezichten zijn als galjoenen
geloogd door handen die eeuwen pagaaiden
stroomopwaarts—mijn geliefden hebben roerloos gekoerst
naar hun kusten mijn moeder

het duel met de wind is als spiegels
die breken het zoeklicht
naar god
om de nacht te ontmaskeren zijn schepen verbrand
en de regen rent naakt achter mij

waar jij doolt waait op het stof
het verstopt onze nadagen
het heult met de zon

wij liggen verankerd—mijn moeder
mijn voet is zeewaardig en
de bruggen staan open en
de zeilen staan bol
wij zijn niet afgedreven—geen ogenblik
gehavend zijn wij

wend niet het gezicht af—mijn moeder
ook ik ben stukgewaaid maar
afstand krimpt en er is geen ruimte zonder jou

[ZIJ ZIEN ONS VERGAAN ALS MISLUKTE OOGST]

zij zien ons vergaan als mislukte oogst
schudden de christelijke hoofden
wij zwijgen als velden
jammeren niet
gij hebt het gedaan
zien verbaasd elkaar in de ogen
hijgen in de smog van verval

ASTRID ROEMER (1947)

[DON'T TURN YOUR FACE AWAY—MY MOTHER]

don't turn your face away—my mother
I too am broken by the wind but
distance shrinks and there is no space without you

the seven seas have been sailed
twisting paths explored—alas
my vistas are like galleons
shaped by hands that for centuries paddled
upstream—my loved ones have followed a rudderless course
to their coasts my mother

the duel with the wind is like mirrors
that break the searchlight
for god
to unmask the night ships have been burned
and the rain runs naked behind me

where you roam dust rises
it hides our declining years
it colludes with the sun

we lie anchored—my mother
my foot is seaworthy and
the bridges are open and
the sails are swelling
we have not been adrift—not for one moment
battered or torn

don't turn your face away—my mother
I too am broken by the wind but
distance shrinks and there is no space without you

tr. Myra Scholz

[THEY SEE US PERISHING AS FAILED HARVEST]

they see our perishing as failed harvest
shake their christian heads
we are silent as fields
do not complain
thou hast done it
look surprised in each other's eyes
pant in the smog of decay

Laten Wij Liefhebben
Laten Wij Liefhebben

trouble in mind cry me the blues sister
blus de hitte van mijn pijn
cover me spread your love all over me brother
hoofden vol vlechten en krullen
onthullen de zalvende schijn
stir it up stir it up people
laten we verstrengeld moisty en hot
samen de laatste plebejers zijn
we are the toughest we are the toughest
Laten We Nobelnaakt Maar Nooit Bang Zijn

be black and be proud
brult de panter in afrika
uhuru, jankt mijn ziel
white christmas lord a wonderful white world
rinkelt santa claus in het westen
uhuru, jankt mijn ziel

Laten Wij Liefhebben
ziet naar de bijen en de bloemen
hun vrede is de vrijheid van hun groei
naar de sterren lonken ze, heel de aarde omarmen ze
want onuitputtelijk en waardevast is hun goud

Wij Blijven Beminnen
adam en eva, vitaal en rusteloos
HEIL RACISTEN—dat onze goden u welgezind zijn
wij sterven van overgave
hebben onze vijanden zelfs gevoed

Wij Blijven Beminnen
ontwortelden-gearresteerden-gemartelden-onderworpenen
analfabeten-daklozen
wij offeren voor het dagelijks brood van hongerenden en
vergeven de uitbuiters van flora en fauna
wij vertolken het paradigmavreemd persoonlijk leed

Laten Wij Liefhebben
ziet naar de bijen en de bloemen
dansen ze niet vrij in de wind ongestoord zoemend
hun onbegrepen aria's en ons is de liefde die verdampt
uit hun adem: JEZUS MAAR HOE BLOEDT MIJN RECHTERWANG

Let Us Love One Another
Let Us Love One Another

trouble in mind cry me the blues sister
put out the heat of my flame
cover me spread your love all over me brother
heads full of braids and curls
throw off the smooth facade
stir it up stir it up people
entangled moisty and hot let us
together be the last plebeians
we are the toughest we are the toughest
Let Us Be Nobly Naked But Never Afraid

be black and be proud
roars the panther in africa
uhuru, howls my soul
white christmas lord a wonderful white world
jingles santa claus in the west
uhuru, howls my soul

Let Us Love One Another
consider the birds and the bees
their peace is their freedom to grow
with eyes on the stars all the earth they embrace
for their gold never fails and its value is sure

We Keep On Loving
adam and eve, restless with life
HAIL RACISTS—that our gods may be kind to you
we die of devotion
have even kept our enemies fed

We Keep On Loving
the uprooted-arrested-tortured-oppressed
illiterate-homeless
we sacrifice for the daily bread of the hungry and
forgive the exploiters of flora and fauna
our tale is of personal grief beyond every paradigm.

Let Us Love One Another
consider the bees and the birds
don't they dance free in the wind buzzing unbothered
their uncomprehended arias and the love they breathe out
is for us: BUT CHRIST HOW MY RIGHT CHEEK IS BLEEDING

tr. Myra Scholz

DE REIGERS VAN AMSTERDAM, DE HERTOGIN EN DE ZEBRA'S

De hertogin had al haar rijpaarden losgelaten in de Amsterdamse
    stadsparken
maar omdat ze zich daarna nog weemoediger voelde dan voorheen
was ze naar Artis gefietst en had met de oppasser van de zebra's
    een dealtje gemaakt:
Elke keer als ze zich melancholiek voelde mocht ze een ritje
    komen maken.
Denkt u dat ie het wel wil? vroeg ze en streelde met een witkanten
    gehandschoende hand de nek van een zebrahengst
daarna keek ze snel of z'n zwarte strepen niet hadden afgegeven.
Wat, riep de oppasser, wat, niet één, wel tien kunt u er krijgen.
Poeh, zei de hertogin. Ze liep op haar tenen langs de zebra's en
    lokte ze een beetje
arme zebra's, dacht ze, wat een rot leven op dat kleine stukje grond.
Zal ik een gedicht voor ze voorlezen, vroeg ze.
Alstublieft, antwoordde de oppasser, een liefdesgedicht.

Lieve zebra, zachte engel, streepdier met je mooie oren
wil je m'n gedicht wel horen
zal ik je vertellen over de wind die over de steppen waait
over het wijde land, over het gras dat nooit wordt gemaaid
over de zebra-merries die glanzend voorbij hollen
over hun sterke benen en hun achterwerken, mooier dan van de
mooiste snollen

Ik weet het verder niet meer, zei ze
helemaal verlegen omdat de oppasser haar met open mond van top
    tot teen stond te bekijken.
Zoals in de meeste gedichten het geval is begon het zijdezacht
te regenen.
Laten we de zebra's naar binnen drijven stelde de hertogin voor.
Toen ze klaar waren groette de hertogin ten afscheid.
Ciao.
Daarna racete ze op haar fiets door de stad
opgejaagd door de muziek van Queen in de hoofdtelefoon
en door het heimwee naar al die zachte aanrakingen van de zebra's
Marquerita Marquerita zong het in haar oren;

CARLA BOGAARDS (1947)

THE HERONS OF AMSTERDAM, THE DUCHESS AND THE ZEBRAS

The duchess set her riding horses free in Amsterdam's park
but because she felt more melancholy than ever
she bicycled to Artis and made a deal with the zebra keeper:*
whenever she felt sad she could come for a ride.
Do you think this one would like it? she asked, patting the neck of a zebra
    stallion with a hand gloved in white lace,
then quickly looking to see if his black stripes had rubbed off.
What! Just one? cried the caretaker. You can have more, you can have ten!
Ooh, said the duchess. She tip-toed to the zebras and cooed softly to them.
Poor zebras, she thought, what a terrible life on that little piece of ground.
Shall I read them a poem? she asked.
Please, answered the caretaker, a love poem.

Dear zebra, soft angel, striped creature with beautiful ears
would you like to hear my poem,
shall I tell you about the wind blowing over the plains,
about the wide open land, about the grass never mown,
about the zebra mares running by, shining bright,
about their strong legs and beautiful rears,
more beautiful than the most beautiful ladies of the night

The rest I don't know, she said, suddenly shy
because the caretaker was staring at her from head to toe
    with his mouth open.
Then, as is customary in most poems, a satin-soft rain began to fall.
Let's take the zebras inside, the duchess suggested.
When they finished the duchess said,
Ciao.
Then she raced on her bicycle through the city
with a shocking rock tune by Queen on her headphones
and as she remembered softly touching the zebras
the music sang in her ears: *Marquerita Marquerita.*

* Artis is Amsterdam's public zoo.

dat was haar eigen tekst
Marquerita Marquerita, de schilderes die altijd veegjes blauwe
    verf aan haar tengere vingers meedroeg.
De hertogin racete op haar fiets door de stad
naar het atelier van de queen of the blues
die zou haar troosten en omhelzen.

Marquerita Marquerita schreven vijf reigers met hun snavel
in de waterplassen op de stoepen rondom de stopera.

TAAL

Wat ik denk en voel zit opgesloten
binnen de kille muren van een vreemde taal.
Het wil naar buiten door de kieren
tussen grammaticale regels,
doorheen het sleutelgat
van een verborgen betekenis.
Iedere gevangene koestert nog
de hoop om ooit weer vrij te zijn.
Voor mij is er alleen maar vrijheid
in een verhoopte andere wereld,
waar de talen overvloeien in elkaar,
waar svobodá precies hetzelfde betekent
als vrijheid,
waar hoop precies hetzelfde is
als nadézjda,
en vaderland en rodína verwijzen
naar iedere plek op deze aarde.

Those were her own words,
Marquerita, Marquerita, the woman painter who always had blue paint
    on the tips of her slender fingers.
The duchess raced on her bicycle through the city
to the studio of the queen of the blues
who would console and embrace her.

With their sharp bills five herons wrote Marquerita Marquerita
in the water puddles on the steps around the Stopera.*

tr. J. H. and J. W. Prins

MAJA PANAJOTOVA (1951)

LANGUAGE

What I think and feel is enclosed
in the bleak walls of a foreign language.
It wants to get out through the cracks
between the grammatical rules,
out through the keyhole
of a hidden meaning.
Every prisoner keeps nursing
a hope to be free once again.
For me there is only freedom
in a yearned-for other world,
where languages flow into one another,
where svobodá means exactly the same
as freedom
where hope is exactly the same
as nadézjda,
and fatherland and rodína refer
to every spot on this earth.

tr. Sheila Gogol and Erica Eijsker

---

* Stopera is an elision of the words *stadhuis en opera*. It refers to the building in Amsterdam
that serves as both city hall and music theater.

[STRAKS KOMT HET SNEEUWEN]

straks komt het sneeuwen
en lopen haar voetsporen vol
vrolijk wit, maar
ook dat is zelfbedrog zoals
het reizen, het hopen op een toeval

straks sneeuwt alles onder:
de sporen van de tram,
de voeten waarmee
ze naar je toe kon gaan
de kinderwagens
de ruitewissers

[ZE WOU DAT ZE IETS TERUGVOND]

ze wou dat ze iets terugvond,
een verlaten binnenhof, gestolen geld
een handschoen waarin nog warmte over
dat ze iets herkende: de geur op de trap
de verschoten kleuren van de gevels

ze wou het liever niet alleen
op de trein, op de roltrap, in de straten
schuin tegen het sneeuwen in

ze wou liever storm op zee
en niet verdwalen

MIRIAM VAN HEE (1952)

[LATER ON THE SNOW WILL COME]

later on the snow will come
and her footprints will be
filled with cheerful white, but
even that is self-deception like
traveling, hoping for a coincidence

later on the snow will cover all:
the tramway tracks,
the feet she could have used
to come to you
the baby carriages
the windshield wipers

> *tr. Marjolijn de Jager*

[SHE WISHED SHE COULD RECOVER SOMETHING]

she wished she could recover something,
a deserted courtyard, stolen money
a glove still warm, so she might recognize
something: the odor on the stairs
the faded colors of the gables

she would rather not have it alone
on the train, on the escalator, in the streets,
leaning forward in the snow

she would rather have a storm at sea
and not get lost

> *tr. Ria Loohuizen*

IN DE PASKAMER VAN V&D

Terwijl ik mij geroutineerd
Een BH omgord, cup C
Maar nee, te klein
Toch maar weer 80 D
Hoor ik twee vrouwenstemmen
Die sussend en bezwerend
Een meisje initiëren

Nee, zo je hand erin, iets scheef
Geef dan een rukje naar het midden
Nu weer omhoog, daarna druk je ze
Op de juiste wijze in het cupje

Twee vrouwen sjorren aan haar borsten
Rennen af en aan met maten
En in het gesprek vallen gaten
Waarin een klein geluid, een zwak protest
Van een gekwetst kind, behandeld als vee
"Deze vind ik niet mooi, nee, nee,"

En ik herinner mij de winkel
Van Hunkemöller Lexis
Die nog steeds een besmette plek is
Vanwege die vreemde handen
Waardoor ik mij nerveus bezweet
Gewillig liet betasten en ik weet
Nu nog hoe mijn stem stierf in mijn keel

The New Savages (1987–)

INEKE VAN MOURIK

IN THE DRESSING ROOM OF THE DEPARTMENT STORE

As I routinely try on
A bra, size C
But no, too small,
Back to D,
I overhear the whispers
Of two women
At a young girl's fitting

No, sideways with your hand, and now
Tug to the middle and then up
Again and this is how
You push them into the cup

Two women handling her breasts
Run back and forth with other sizes
And in the gaps between I hear
A small sound, the weak protest
Of a now harnessed child
"No, I don't like this one either,"

And I remember the store
Called Hunkemöller Lexis
Which is still a haunted spot
Because of those strange hands
That I let touch me, in nervous sweat
But willing, and even now I feel
My voice dying in my throat

    tr. J. H. and J. W. Prins

PRINSJESDAG

wijd als een tent
staat haar gewaad
stijf van brocaatzijden isolement

middelbare vrouwen
even het aardappelmesje in rust
met witte tassen en regenjassen
samengedreven achter hekken
in de hoop op een prins die ze wakkerkust
juichen en zwaaien
laten zich door haar glimlach verrassen
hun moederhart in lichterlaaie

terwijl zij toch zoëven
met haar stem van lispelend platina
haar staalblauwe oogleden
haar mond uit Wassenaar
Gods hulp heeft afgebeden
ten behoeve van verkilde heren

zegen hun roverswerk, o Heer
zie op hun onbarmhartigheid neer
in 's Lands belang mag wie arm is creperen

zij staat in haar eenzaamheid op het balkon
toegejuicht door haar getrouwen
zij is een hoer van Babylon
in plaats van de hoogste der vrouwen

o zuster, laat je niet langer onteren

EVA VAN SONDEREN (1948)

PRINCE DAY*

wide like a tent
her gown of silk brocade
stands in stiff detachment

middle-aged housewives
potato peelers left behind
clutching white purses, dressed for rain
driven behind barricades
hoping for a prince to kiss them awake
they cheer and wave
pleased to receive a smile from her
warming the heart of any mother

while she just now
with her voice of lisping platinum
her steely blue eyelids
her upper-class lips
has prayed to God
on behalf of cold-blooded gentlemen

blessed be their work of thievery,
O Lord, sanction their cruelty
let the poor starve for the sake of our country

alone she stands on the balcony
while the faithful crowds are cheering
she is the whore of Babylon
and not the most respected of women

O sister, do not let this lie go on

tr. J. H. and J. W. Prins

---

* Prince Day (Prinsjesdag) is the third Tuesday of September. After her traditional tour in the golden carriage— through the Hague—the queen arrives at the House of Commons, where she holds her yearly speech on the government policy for the coming year. This poem is on—and in the end addressed to—Queen Beatrix.

[ALS MANNEN ZOUNDEN BLOEDEN]

als mannen zouden bloeden
hoe groot en imposant het maandverband
in de toiletten extra ruimte
en stickers op de autoramen
niet passeren—kramp

als mannen kinderen zouden baren
dan was de pil verguld
baby's huilden door de intercom van directeuren
en secretaressen, die luiers moesten wassen,
werden geselecteerd op het criterium geduld

als mannen kinderen moesten zogen
hadden ze dan tijd voor oorlog en geweld
zouden ze nog zoveel vergaderen en zeuren
ja zeuren blijft hetzelfde, ze zouden zeggen
nee mens geen oorlog nu—ik ben ongesteld

[MIJN LIEF, IK VAAR EEN SCHIP VOL TRANEN]

mijn lief, ik vaar een schip vol tranen
een schip vol tranen naar je toe
ik had wat anders willen brengen
vertel me wat je wilt en hoe

ik je geweven innigheid kan geven
of vreugde in een doosje van karton
of flesjes zonlicht van de eerste morgen
of alle bergen die je ooit beklom

dat alles in een sloep van goede tijden
ze vaart wel mee maar is nog onder zeil

en voor ik al die schatten kan bevrijden
moet eerst dit vaartuig schipbreuk lijden

vooruit sirene, blaas de stormwind aan
als ik bij jou ben durf ik wel vergaan.

CHAWWA WIJNBERG (1942)

[IF MEN COULD BLEED]

if men could bleed
how important their sanitary needs
their bathrooms extra large, with ramps,
and bumper stickers on their cars would read
no passing—menstrual cramps

if men brought children into the world
the pill would be enshrined in gold
babies would cry on the office intercom
and secretaries hired not for filing papers
but for their patience in washing diapers

if men nursed babies at the breast
would they still have time for wars and violence
would they still complain at every conference
yes of course, complain they certainly would
they'd say—no war right now, I'm getting my period

tr. J. H. and J. W. Prins

[MY LOVE, A SHIP FULL OF TEARS]

my love, a ship full of tears
a ship of tears I sail to you
I would have brought something else
tell me what you want and how

to give you a tapestry of tenderness
or joy in cardboard packages
or flasks of sunlight from the first morning
or all the mountains you ever climbed

all in a sloop bringing better times
a sloop that's sailing far behind

and before those treasures can be found
first this ship must run aground

come siren, blow the stormwind, blow
once I reach you I'll let go.

tr. J. H. and J. W. Prins

[STEL DAT WIJ VAN ATLANTIS KWAMEN]

Stel dat wij van Atlantis kwamen
ons land en erfgoed vergaan
stel dat we over de wereld dwaalden
geen Palestina om naar terug te gaan

stel we hadden geen boeken om te bestuderen
geen Roots om naar op zoek te gaan
stel we waren onze taal verloren
geen mogelijkheid meer elkaar te verstaan

stel we leefden al eeuwen als ballingen
nooit bij elkaar, altijd apart
stel men verachtte ons op deze aarde
verkocht ons, mishandelde ons, verkrachtte ons

stel men behandelde ons als beesten
als aaipoes, als werkvee, voor de fok
stel men zou onze opstand negeren
onze daden vergeten, ontkend, bespot

stel men zou ons doden, kastijden,
verbranden, verminken, in stukken snijden
stel men zou ons bezingen en schilderen
ons symbool maken van zonde en lust

stel we waren van alles afgesneden
van heden, toekomst en verleden
Wat zou dit dan voor wereld zijn

ANNEMARIE DE WAARD (1944)

[SUPPOSE WE CAME FROM ATLANTIS]

Suppose we came from Atlantis
without our land and inheritance
suppose we wandered all over the world
no Palestine where we might return

suppose we had no books to read
no Roots to seek and rediscover
suppose we lost all our words
no way to understand each other

suppose we lived as exiles centuries long
never together, always alone
suppose everyone on earth despised us
sold and raped and abused us

suppose people treated us like animals
for petting or as labor or to breed
suppose our revolution was negated
our deeds forgotten, denied, and hated

suppose people punished and killed us
burned, maimed, slashed us into pieces
suppose people slurred and mocked us
made us symbols of sin and lust

suppose we were denied all things that last
cut off from the present, the future and the past
what kind of a world then would this be

   tr. J. H. and J. W. Prins

AAN DE KADE STAAT EEN HUIS

Waar Zij niet heerst, de
harde Passie, heerst het Huisgezin.
(In welke vorm dan ook.)

Daar hangen broeken te drogen daar
staan pannen eten bewaard te worden—
tot morgen, tot overmorgen, daar
kan alles wachten.

DE GEMS

In de hoge Alpen
spring ik van rots naar rots.
Nu zei mij een lesbienne
—niet zonder trots—
Zoals jij springt, Gems, ga ik
van geliefde naar geliefde.

Ik voelde mededogen, maar ook
griefde mij dit vergelijken.
Haar liefdes! Bitter. Heftig. Kort van duur.
Mijn sprongen! Simpel. Krachtig. Puur.

BABETTE

Babette Babette jij kijkt mij aan
Babette je kan niet mee.
Het nylon plooit gedwee in de
advertentie.
Model Babette. Liefde onvervuld.
Babette in nylon. Babette gehuld.
Ik moet niet zo denken.
Ik mag niet zo zijn.
Maar met Babette—lijkt het mij fijn.

SJUUL DECKWITZ (1952)

ON THE QUAYSIDE STANDS A HOUSE

Where She reigns not,
the Queen of Passion,
household matters smother.

Where leftover food is hoarded
until tomorrow, until next week,
where laundry hangs to dry,
there, Passion can but die.

tr. Rina Vergano, in collaboration with the author

THE MOUNTAIN GOAT

In the Alpine mountains
As I leapt from crag to crag
I chanced upon a lesbian
And proudly did she brag:
"As you leap, my agile brother,
So I flit from lover to lover."

This comparison left me vexed
But her bragging touched my heart.
Her loves! Here one moment, gone the next.
My leaps! Simple, strong and smart.

tr. Rina Vergano, in collaboration with the author

BABETTE

Babette Babette you look at me
Captive of the catalog.
Your shorty nightie billows meekly
on page 33.
Lingerie Babette. Love unrequited.
With your nylon covered curves
I can never be united.
Mustn't think like this.
What's come over me?
Lingerie Babette, promise of ecstasy.

tr. Rina Vergano, in collaboration with the author

ZIJ HUILT. ZIJ LACHT.

Zij had twee liefdes en heeft hen verloren.
Vlak na elkaar.
Zij schreide zich onmachtig,
blondeerde heur haar,
sloop, vol doodsgedachten,
langs kleine, louche grachten.
Clara! Emilie?
Zwijgen was haar evenknie.

Zie haar nu lachen naar Evelien—
Nog twee jaar. Dàn zal de gracht
haar schreien weer zien.

WIJ ZIJN NACHTDYNAMO'S

Zeven jaren her gingen we ver,
werden nooit ziek—
zo vaak weerklonk: naar tante Riek!

In het grauwe ochtendgloren
trok de massa naar kantoren
en zongen we een lied.
Slapen? Wij niet—en van je hela.

Nu, op een bankje langs de dansvloer,
hand in hand, lispelen we als sijsjes
en staren, uitgeblust, naar wilde jonge meisjes.

SHE CRIES. SHE LAUGHS.

She had two loves and lost them.
In quick succession.
She cried herself senseless,
bleached her hair,
trailed along narrow, seedy gutters,
entertaining thoughts of death,
bewailing Claribel and Gert.
Silence was her just desert.

Now see her smile at sweet Elaine—
Two years from now
she will be crying in the gutter once again.

tr. Rina Vergano, in collaboration with the author

WE ARE NIGHT DYNAMOS

Seven years ago, come rain, come snow,
we were never laid low
nightly did our battle-cry resound
Come! Let us hasten to the Hare and Hound!

In the ashy light of day
the office crowd was underway
while we sang out our carol:
Sleep? Who needs it!—Roll out the barrel!

Now, hand in hand, on a sofa by the dance floor
we sit and twitter like two budgies in a cage
and stare, exhausted, at the wild, young dancing girls
half our age.

tr. Rina Vergano, in collaboration with the author

ENDNOTES

1. According to Ria Lemaire (1988) this dawn poem has to be understood against the backdrop of Indo-European marriage customs. An "abduction"—planned beforehand by the lovers—was considered the lowest form of the four types of marriage practiced at the time. Since other marriage forms were more dignified, the young woman can say, "Ic ligge in mijns liefs armkens Met grooter waerdicheyt" (I lie in my lief's arms with greater *dignity*"). The young woman receives word that her lover has been killed by his rival. The body lies "under the green linden," the linden (lime tree) being the symbolic place for lovers' meetings. The young woman takes her mantle, that is, she invests herself with her official status and dignity of noblewoman. She arranges for the burial, demanding that her kin officially acknowledge her relationship with this dead man, which also implies revenge for the murder. The silence of the knights is terrible.

Lemaire interprets the tension as a dramatization of the conflict between the first and the second stage of feudal society. The young woman's behavior shows her to be a conscious proponent of the old custom, which allowed for various types of marriage. Women still had the right to choose. The father and the knights represent the transition to the more hierarchical organization of the extended family under a *paterfamilias*, where only one monogamous marriage form is left and the father decides. The terrible silence signifies the transition from one historical stage to the other. The father is embarrassed, unable to give his daughter an outright no or to confront her directly. See Ria Lemaire, "Dubbel gelijk of driedubbel ongelijk—overdenkingen bij een hedendaagse interpretatie van 'Het daghet inden Oosten,'" in *Door het oog van de tekst: Essays voor Mieke Bal over visie,* ed. E. van Alphen en I. de Jong (Muiderberg: Coutinho, 1988), 85–105.

2. "The Song of the Plow" was written down as sung by women in the nineteenth century, although it is probably much older. A number of versions are known, originating in different parts of the country. This version stems from Dongen, near Breda, at that time a poor rural area in the southern part of The Netherlands. Songs of this kind, warning against male brutality and celebrating women's power, were sung at the traditional all-women's evenings known as "spinningen," when unmarried women got together to spin wool and sing. Around 1900 such evenings were taken over by male musicians. Source: Ate Doorenbosch, "Onder de groene linde," radio program.

3. Discussions on the interpretation of this poem continue. The most recent editors (Sneller and Van Marion 1994) of Tesselschade's collected poems think that she went to bed with the captain, since lovemaking was often

described as the laying down of one's armor. Tesselschade would then be pointing out that she does not wish to follow up on this little adventure.

It is remarkable that Tesselschade, in comparing the captain with Delilah and herself with Samson, reverses the sex roles of the story. Delilah seduced Samson for the sake of finding out the secret of his strength. This female Samson is only too willing to disclose her secret: her strength is in her steel! The sex reversal is given additional stress in the translation, where Tesselschade represents herself as armed with a "spear."

4. This poem exploits the conventions of Petrarchan love lyric. Typically in a poem of this kind a male persona praises his lady's beauty, ending with the lament that her heart is hard as a diamond, cold as ice. Questiers's poem starts from there: her female persona teases her ardent suitor by saying that her icy "diamond" should stay where it is. See Myra Scholz-Heerspink, "Reflections on Translating, Theory, Meter, Rhyme and Three Dutch Poems," in *Something Understood: Studies in Anglo-Dutch Literary Translation,* Bart Westerweel and Theo D'haen, eds. (Amsterdam: Rodopi, 1990), 291–304.

5. Myriam Everard comments on this poem: "De liefde van Lesbos in Nederland," *Tijdschrift voor Vrouwenstudies* 5 (1984) 3:339. I also thank my colleague Prof. Dr. Lia van Gemert for her comments on this poem.

6. The poet H. A. Spandaw (1777–1855) wrote a reply to this poem. With a variant on each line he defends the proposition that nature prefers fair over dark.

7. Before her "Boston marriage" to Betje Wolff-Bekker, Deken was romantically involved with Maria Bavinck and with the poet Maria Bosch, who died very young. On "Boston marriages" between women see Lillian Faderman, *Surpassing the Love of Men: Romantic Friendship and Love Between Women from the Renaissance to the Present* (New York: William Morrow, 1981).

NOTES ON THE POETS

ANNA BIJNS (1493–1575) was born in Antwerp, Belgium, where she spent her entire life. She opened her own school, earning her living as a teacher until she was eighty years old. Bijns published several volumes of poems known as *Refereynen* (Refrains) and was deeply immersed in the literary, religious, and political life of her time. As a committed Roman Catholic she vehemently opposed the Reformation. Bijns was the first woman in Dutch literary history to write openly about sexual desire, which led to predictable prejudices among later male interpreters. She also wrote religious, socially critical, and humorous poetry. Bijns is one of the most important poets of the early sixteenth century, and her work is still surprisingly readable. In 1985 a major prize for the female voice in Dutch literature was named after Bijns.

KATHARINA WILHELMINA BILDERDIJK-SCHWEICKHARDT (1777–1830) spent her youth in England, during which time she demonstrated great talent for drawing, poetry, and needlework. She started writing in English and later produced work in French and Italian as well. Besides being a writer she worked as a translator and studied Eastern languages. Her husband, Willem Bilderdijk, the greatest Dutch poet of the time, published her poems in his own volumes.

ANNA BLAMAN (1905–1960), pseudonym for Jo Vrugt, wrote stories and novels that reflect a general disenchantment with life after the Second World War. Heavily influenced by French existentialism, she portrayed people as being utterly alone, victims of a human condition that even erotic love is powerless to change. Blaman's novels, especially *Eenzaam Avontuur* (*Lonesome Adventure,* 1948), created a scandal because of their explicit representation of lesbian love. Like Andreas Burnier after her, Blaman pioneered in bringing this subject to the awareness of postwar Dutch society. Although labeled immoral by some contemporaries, Blaman's work is intensely concerned with ethical values.

CARLA BOGAARDS (1947) writes poetry and prose, as well as short theater pieces in which she also performs, accompanied on cello by a friend. Love is central to her work: "love for friends, for my lover, for children, for elderly people," as she says. Underlying all her work is the desire to show that women do have power. Bogaards is well known as a performing poet.

ANDREAS BURNIER (C. I. Dessaur) (1931) was one of the leading radical lesbians of the early seventies. She is a poet, novelist, heterodox feminist, philosopher, professor of criminology, and contributor to several seminal public debates in The Netherlands (on euthanasia, for example). Her novels, *Een tevreden lach (A Satisfied Laugh), Het jongensuur (The Boys' Hour), De huilende libertijn (The Weeping Libertine), De reis naar Kithira (Journey to Kithira),* and *De literaire salon (The Literary Salon)* have greatly enhanced the cultural visibility of lesbianism in The Netherlands. The main characters in these stories often lead a rather tormented lesbian existence, feeling caught in a woman's body and haunted by memories of a higher, nonphysical world of light and peace. After producing a series of books inspired by Neoplatonist, Buddhist, and Jungian spirituality, she rediscovered Jewish religion and culture. Burnier's latest novel, *De Wereld is van glas (The Glass World),* contains a moving account of the time she spent in hiding as a child during the Second World War.

SJUUL DECKWITZ (1952) made her debut with *Onwetende vampieren (Ignorant Vampires,* 1980), poems published under the pseudonym of Annette Wanrooy, "a troubled thirty-year-old lesbian who seeks her comfort in magazines, poetry, short romances, and alcohol." Using certain Amsterdam circles as a source of inspiration, Deckwitz conjures up the decadent side of the lesbian scene. Her poems, comics, and short stories are at the same time extremely funny, sad, absurd, and romantic. Deckwitz also published two novels: *God aan het IJ (God at the River IJ,* 1993) and *Gelijk de zee (Like the Sea,* 1995).

ERIKA DEDINSZKY (1942) was born in Budapest and then moved to The Netherlands as a child. She studied French, philosophy, and Hungarian, and stimulated awareness of Hungarian culture in The Netherlands with her translations. Dedinszky has published two volumes of poetry in Dutch, *Kornoeljeboom (Dogwood Tree,* 1975) and *De ijstijd begint met de kou (The Ice-Age Starts with the Cold,* 1980). She received the Martinus Nijhoff Prize for her translations in 1981. She currently works as a translator.

AGATHA DEKEN (1741–1804), see ELIZABETH WOLFF-BEKKER

CHRISTINE D'HAEN (1923), a Flemish poet, studied Dutch, English, and German. She worked for many years teaching English and as keeper of the Gezelle archives. D'haen also wrote a biography of Guido Gezelle, the important Flemish priest-poet who died in 1899, and translated his poetry into English. Her own lyrical work owes its complexity and richness to motifs drawn from a variety of cultures (classical Greek, Arabic, Indian). Two recent volumes of her poetry are *Mirages* (1989) and *Morgane* (1995). D'haen also writes beautiful prose, as in *Zwarte sneeuw (Black Snow,* 1989). She has received several prizes for her poetry, including the Anna Bijns Prize in 1991 and the Prijs der Nederlandse Letteren in 1992.

CHRISTA EELMAN (unknown) published only one volume of feminist poetry, in 1981, *Over niet meer kunnen (When You Can't Go On)*. Difficulties in relationships—between men and women, but also between mothers and daughters—are the main theme of her poems.

CLARA EGGINK (1906–1991) worked as a journalist and critic all her life, in addition to writing poetry. Her early marriage to the Dutch poet J. C. Bloem in 1932 ended after six years, but the couple was reunited in 1959. She wrote a beautiful memoir of her life with Bloem after his death. Her most interesting poems were written mainly in the 1930s and early 1940s. Her collection entitled *De rand van de horizon (The Edge of the Horizon,* 1954) was reprinted in 1994. The recent revival of interest in Eggink has also resulted in a well-researched story of her life (Lucy Vermij, *Ik stortte mij over de grenzen: Leven en werk van Clara Eggink*) (*Headlong Across Borders: Life and Work of Clara Eggink*).

ANNA ENQUIST (1945), after a musical career as a pianist, became a psychotherapist and, in her late thirties, a remarkable poet. Enquist's first volume, *Soldatenliederen (Soldiers' Songs,* 1991) was a literary sensation. This poet seemed to be producing classical work from her very first line. Since then Enquist has published two more volumes of poetry (in 1992 and 1994) and two novels.

ELISABETH EYBERS (1915), originally from Transvaal, South Africa, has lived in Amsterdam since 1961. Her mother tongue was English, her father's native language Afrikaans. She continued to write poetry in Afrikaans after coming to The Netherlands. She was awarded three of the most prestigious Dutch literary prizes: the Herman Gorter Prize (1974), the Constantijn Huygens Prize (1978) and the P. C. Hooft Prize (1991). Her *Versamelde gedigte (Collected Poems)* were published in 1990, followed by new volumes, *Respyt (Respite,* 1993), *Nuweling (Newcomer,* 1995), and *Tijdverdryf (Pastime)* in 1996. Eybers's poetry can be characterized as a series of meditations on everyday life, on relations with friends and the beloved, and—in old age—on the frailty of the body.

IDA GERHARDT (1905–1997) is an important poet and translator of the classics (the Psalms, Lucretius, Virgil). She worked as a teacher of Latin and Greek until early retirement. Gerhardt produced an extensive poetic oeuvre of classic, sometimes archaic beauty. Her poems contain many echoes of Biblical language. Although the tone is often lofty and prophetic, it is also highly personal. Gerhardt always kept aloof from the male modernists in Dutch poetry, working more in the tradition of older poets like Leopold, Boutens, Bloem, Henriette Roland Holst and even Sappho. She received the P. C. Hooft Prize in 1979. Despite deteriorating eyesight she continued to write until a few years before her death in 1997.

HELLA S. HAASSE (1918) was born in Batavia (Jakarta) in the former Dutch East Indies. Her Indonesian experiences have been a source of inspiration, from her first novel *Oeroeg* (1948) to her most recent one, *Heren van de thee* (*The Tea Merchants*, 1992). She brought medieval, Renaissance, and eighteenth-century history to life in a wide range of well-researched historical novels. Her work has been widely translated and is very popular in The Netherlands. Haasse has published relatively little poetry; after her promising debut as a poet, with *Stroomversnelling* (*Rapids*, 1945), she focused on the historical novel, autobiography, and essay. She has received a number of awards, including the Constantijn Huygens Prize in 1981, and the prestigious P. C. Hooft Prize in 1983.

HADEWIJCH (13th century) is known as the greatest Dutch poet of the thirteenth century. Very little is known about her life, but fortunately much of her work has survived. Her poems about "Minne" (Love) are rooted in deep mystical experiences and express an intense striving for unity between God and the human soul. Hadewijch often used a fixed stanzaic form. She also wrote a startling series of prose visions. Her letters to the circle of religious women whom she served as spiritual leader have survived as well. Hadewijch's *Complete Works* have been translated into English by Mother Columba Hart (London: SPCK, 1981).

FRITZI TEN HARMSEN VAN DER BEEK (1927), already a cult poet before the publication of her first book, *Geachte muizenpoot en andere gedichten* (*Venerable Mouse-leg and Other Poems*, 1965), writes highly original texts—absurdist, desperate, yet of great technical intricacy. Her second volume, *Kus of ik schrijf* (*Kiss or Else I'll Write*, 1975) also deals with loss and decay, but in an extremely humorous way. Although Harmsen van Beek has published some remarkable prose as well, she remains the author of a small but beloved poetic oeuvre.

MIRIAM VAN HEE (1952) is a Flemish poet who made her debut with *Het karige maal* (*The Scanty Meal*) in 1978. Since then she has published several other volumes of poetry. As a Slavist, Van hee has also translated Russian poetry. She has developed her own symbolic language, in which "snow," "winter," "bike," and "train" are important semantic fields.

JUDITH HERZBERG (1934) was immediately recognized as a subtle and important poet with the publication of her first book of poems *Zeepost* (*Surface Mail*, 1963). In her work the seemingly small things in everyday existence turn out to be mirrors of life's complexity. Besides her nine volumes of poetry, Herzberg has written film scripts and plays, which have provided an important impetus to Dutch film and theater production. The play *Leedvermaak* (*Malicious Joy*, 1982) deals with the way in which the Second World War still haunts a Jewish family forty years later. It received several prizes and was later made into a film. Herzberg received the P. C. Hooft prize in 1997.

ELISABETH KOOLAERT-HOOFMAN (1664–1736) was born into a wealthy family and received an excellent education. She composed poems in Latin when she was sixteen, but her later oeuvre was mainly written in Dutch. She married the equally well-to-do Peter Koolaert, who wasted their capital on extravagant parties and other luxuries. In 1717, for example, Koolaert received Czar Peter from Russia with a splendor he could not afford. As they ended their lives in poverty, Elisabeth bore her fate with superhuman patience. Most of her work consists of occasional poems.

JULIANA CORNELIA DE LANNOY (1738–1782), a member of a noble family, could afford an education that included the study of English, French, and some Latin. She wrote lyric poems in French classicist style, for which she received several medals of honor from literary societies, as well as tragedies and satire. Willem Bilderdijk and Rhijnvis Feith, the foremost Dutch poets of the time, admired her work. Like her enlightened contemporaries, Betje Wolff-Bekker and Aagje Deken, she consistently promoted equal rights for women, especially the right to education and higher learning.

HANNY MICHAELIS (1922) published her first volume of poems in 1949. With her second volume, *Water uit de rots* (*Water from the Rock,* 1957), her work took on a more modern form. Her poems are often sober, short, and without rhyme. Main themes in her work are melancholy, despair, and (lost) love. A broad selection of her poetry was published in 1989 under the title *Het onkruid van de twijfel (Weeds of Doubt)*. Michaelis received the Anna Bijns Prize in 1995.

NEELTJE MARIA MIN (1944) made her debut as a poet when she was an unwed mother of twenty-one. Her volume *Voor wie ik liefheb wil ik heten (For Those I Love Want to Have a Name)* caught the attention of sensational journalists who began prying into her personal life, doing gross injustice to her work in the process. Her poems were seen as romantic, girlish, and simple, while they are in fact gloomy and vexed, dealing with such somber themes as the imprisonment of a daughter in a family and hatred for the mother. The volume proved to be a huge commercial success, with sales reaching 70,000 copies. Only after twenty years did Min publish another, remarkable, volume, *Een vrouw bezoeken* (*Visiting a Woman,* 1985), followed by new work in 1986 and 1987.

INEKE VAN MOURIK (1949) is one of the founders of the women's bookshop and documentation center De Feeks (The Virago) in Nijmegen. She was an editor of the feminist literary magazine *Lust & Gratie (Lust & Grace)* for fourteen years. Together with others she published the *Lesbisch*

Prachtboek (Lesbian Book of Wonder, 1979), and her novel *Tropenritme (Tropical Rhythm)* appeared in 1988. She is associated with the group of women poets known as De Nieuwe Wilden (The New Savages).

LOES NOBEL (1931) was born in Surabaia, Indonesia, and migrated to The Netherlands when she was twenty-seven. Indonesian culture plays an important role in her work, not only in the themes she chooses, but also in the genres she employs: she revived for example the "wangsalan," a traditional Indonesian poetic form. A prolific poet, Loes Nobel has also published a number of short stories.

NEL NOORDZIJ (1923) published both prose and poetry from 1954 to 1964. Her work was found provocative and shocking because of its explicit treatment of sexuality and the portrayal of neurotic characters in her novels, as in *Het kan me niet schelen (I Don't Care,* 1955). Since 1964 she has published only in the field of psychology, in which she earned a Ph.D. in the United States in 1974.

MAJA PANAJOTOVA (1951) was born in Bulgaria. She studied Slavonic philology in Sofia and Ghent, married a Belgian man, and taught Bulgarian at the universities of Ghent and Louvain. She has been living in Belgium since her marriage, and has translated Dutch literary and academic work into Bulgarian. Panajotova has also published two volumes of poetry, one in Bulgarian, *Da sprem otlitashtata ptitsa (To Stop the Bird in His Flight)* and one in Dutch, *Verzwegen alibi (Hidden Alibi,* 1983).

ANKIE PEYPERS's (1928) first collection of poetry, *Zeventien (Seventeen),* reflecting both her age at the time and the number of poems in the volume, was published in 1946. Her second book, *Oktober (October,* 1951), was followed by many others, including the collection *Gedichten 1951–1975 (Poems, 1951–1975),* published in 1976. Peypers's most recent volume appeared in 1990. She has also written several novels. Peypers is a translator of Latin American poetry and organizes poetry readings and intercultural workshops. She is one of the founders of the Center for Chilean Culture, which cooperates with Latin American writers and artists in exile. She has also set up workshops in creative writing for women. The development of Peypers's poetry testifies to her involvement with the feminist movement as well as with intercontinental literature of our time.

SONJA POS (1936) works as a poet, novelist, essayist, and translator. She lives in Amsterdam and has two sons. Most of her Jewish family was killed in Auschwitz and Sobibor. Pos made her debut in 1963 with *Het efficiënte vergeten (The Efficient Forgetting)* and thus became one of the first Netherlandic Jewish writers to deal with the impossibility of living on after the traumatizing war. In the novel *Daglicht (Daylight,* 1994) she recollects her experience as a young half-Jewish girl during World War II, tracing the process of repression, mourning, and finally, reconciliation with life. Other work by Sonja Pos includes the poetry collection *De eigen tijd* (*Our Own Time,* 1988) and the novel *Een paar woorden per dag* (*A Few Words per Day,* 1985).

KATHARINA QUESTIERS (1631–1669) was praised by her contemporaries as a great poet. Vondel (the most important Dutch poet of the seventeenth century) even called her "a second Sappho." She also wrote several comedies and was talented in sculpture and drawing. After her death the appreciation for her work declined. Only a few of her poems have survived.

GIZA RITSCHL (1869–1942) arrived in The Netherlands at the end of the nineteenth century; she published her first volume of poetry, *Verzen* (*Verses,* 1901), soon after. Willem Kloos, a famous Dutch poet of the time, responded by calling her "the Hungarian Nightingale." Several other volumes followed. Ritschl was known for her free use of meter and her simple style. Love was her main theme.

ASTRID ROEMER (1947), a Dutch author of Surinamese origin, has written poetry, prose, plays, essays, and songs. She was one of the first Dutch writers to focus on the Dutch colonial past and to point out the racism still prevalent in those parts of the world where Dutch is spoken. Another important theme in her work is female sexuality. Roemer writes daring, polemical, baroque texts, using innovative physical and even cosmic imagery to express sexual feelings. Important novels are *Over de gekte van een vrouw* (*A Woman's Madness,* 1982) and *Een naam voor de liefde* (*A Name for Love,* 1990).

ANNA ROEMERS VISSCHER (1584–1651) was the gifted daughter of Roemer Visscher, who was himself a poet. His house was an Amsterdam center of culture, a pleasant meeting point for writers, singers, and painters. Anna received a very modern Renaissance education: she learned French and Italian, and mastered the arts of engraving glass, painting, singing, and playing musical instruments. Among Anna's friends were most of the important Dutch poets of her time. She married late. Her poetry, little of which was published in her lifetime, is often of a serious and religious nature. She also translated French literature into Dutch.

MARIA TESSELSCHADE ROEMERS VISSCHER (1594–1649) was the younger sister of Anna Roemers Visscher. She, too, received a good Renaissance education. "Tesseltje" was often the subject of other poets' poetry (P. C. Hooft in particular devoted many playful poems and letters to her), but of her own often brilliant work very little has survived. She took an active part in the literary life of her time and was a cherished member of the Muider Circle. After the loss of her husband and eldest daughter in 1634, Tesselschade converted to Catholicism.

HENRIETTE ROLAND HOLST-VAN DER SCHALK's (1869–1952) name is inextricably bound to the Dutch proletarian struggle. She was the charismatic leader of the Dutch socialist and communist movements in the first decades of the twentieth century and a key figure on the international socialist scene. Following the initial euphoria of the Russian Revolution, Roland Holst was one of the first prominent communists to recognize the abuse of power and the corruption of the communist system. She acted upon these insights and became an outspoken critic of Stalinist Russia. In later years she turned to a religious and pacifist socialism. In her extensive poetic oeuvre socialist themes are prominent. Her work also shows feminist consciousness: she writes about her struggle against the traditional woman's role, against the passivity and the protected life of the upper-class woman that she was. She also wrote plays, political manifestos, innumerable articles, biographies (of Rousseau, Tolstoy, Rosa Luxemburg, and Gandhi among others), and Marxist studies such as *Kapitaal en arbeid in Nederland (Labour and Capital in The Netherlands)*.

ANNIE M. G. SCHMIDT (1911–1995) is most famous for the prose and poetry she wrote for the very young. Generations of Dutch children have grown up with her unforgettable songs and stories. She also wrote musicals, plays, television series, radio plays, and columns, all of which enjoyed great popularity. Her simple but humorous use of language accounts for the wide accessibility of her work. It was also her inimitable wit that permitted her to break many social and sexual taboos in Dutch society. She especially made fun of bourgeois respectability and boring self-importance. Her poems and songs are collected in *Tot hiertoe (So Far,* 1986). Her work for children has also appeared in a single volume, *Ziezo (There We Are,* 1987).

EVA VAN SONDEREN (1948), daughter of a Jewish mother and a Protestant father, has written on various subjects relating to her cultural roots (on the relation of Dutch Jews to Israel, for example). She has published some poetry and prose in literary magazines and anthologies, and a volume of poetry *Zingend de dag in, en de nacht (Singing into the Day, and the Night,* 1982). She belongs to the group of women poets known as De Nieuwe Wilden (The New Savages). Van Sonderen now lives in Jerusalem, working as a correspondent and social worker, and as a healer in the peace process.

JULIA TULKENS (1902) is a Flemish poet who worked as a teacher for many years. She took an active part in Flemish literary life of the twentieth century, published more than ten volumes of poetry, and received many decorations and awards. Love, fear, and the magical are central to her work.

Her poetry has been translated into six languages. Tulkens's *Verzamelde Gedichten (Collected Poems)* were published in 1978.

ELLY DE WAARD (1940) worked from 1965 to 1984 as a rock critic for two of the most widely read Dutch newspapers, the daily *De Volkskrant* and the weekly *Vrij Nederland.* Her first book of poems, *Afstand (Distance),* appeared in 1978, and her ninth, *Het zij (Or She),* in 1995. Her work developed from the sober, neutral love verses of the first volumes to ecstatic, explicitly lesbian poetry. An exuberant feminist personality, de Waard has been extremely active in literary politics. She was one of the founding members of the Anna Bijns Foundation, which established The Netherlands' most important literary prize for the female voice in literature. She is also the leading figure of the group of female poets, De Nieuwe Wilden (The New Savages), whose works have been collected in two anthologies (see in this volume Eva van Sonderen, Ineke van Mourik, and Chawwa Wijnberg). This movement, which has produced its own manifesto, is perhaps the first of its kind anywhere to focus programmatically on the woman's voice in poetry.

ANNEMARIE DE WAARD (1944), sister of Elly de Waard, has published poetry in several feminist magazines and anthologies, as well as in one volume, *Als Troje (Like Troy,* 1989). She makes use of some older poetic genres— for example, "Geuzenliederen" (Beggar's Songs), originally seventeenth-century protest songs—to which she gives a new feminist content. She is one of the group of women poets known as De Nieuwe Wilden (The New Savages) and works as an independent feminist therapist.

ELLEN WARMOND (1930) published her first poems in the 1950s and has, since then, continued to explore the disturbing themes of existential fear, alienation, and despair. Because her style includes a great deal of personification, the line between the human and nonhuman often becomes blurred. In recent years Warmond's poems have become less ridden with anguish and more philosophical. A selection from her prolific work was published in 1979, as *Tegenspeler Tijd (Opponent Time).* Until her retirement Ellen Warmond worked as assistant curator in the National Museum of Literature in The Hague. She was awarded the Anna Bijns Prize in 1987.

CHAWWA WIJNBERG (1942) works as both a poet and a sculptor. She has had several exhibitions of her work. Jewishness, feminism, and lesbianism are important sources of inspiration for her. Wijnberg is one of the group of women poets known as De Nieuwe Wilden (The New Savages).

ELIZABETH WOLFF-BEKKER (Betje Bekker) (1738–1804) and Agatha Deken (Aagje Deken) (1741–1804) shared a lifelong romantic and creative partnership. Together they wrote a large oeuvre of realist novels, of which

De Historie van Mejuffrouw Sara Burgerhart (*The History of Miss Sara Burgerhart*, 1782), the first modern novel in Dutch literature, is the most famous. Wolff-Bekker and Deken were, in fact, largely responsible for creating the Dutch novel. Both women also wrote poems. Wolff-Bekker and Deken were typical products of the Enlightenment: they pleaded for tolerance and nondogmatic ways of life, and sympathized with the French Revolution. They also produced moralistic and didactic work that expressed their belief in reason as the source of civil virtues. Betje translated several French and English Enlightenment philosophers into Dutch. Her letters are written in a delightful style. As a couple they were inseparable: Aagje died a few days after Betje.

ZARA MARIA VAN ZON (?–1755) is the author of two volumes, *Eeuwgetijde van den Münsterschen Vrede* (*Centennial of the Treaty of Münster,* 1748) and *Eene verzameling van stichtelijke gedichten (A Collection of Devotional Poems),* the second published posthumously. Her posthumous religious poetry was edited by her sister. Zara Maria could voice surprisingly sharp criticism of the poems of male contemporaries.

NOTES ON THE EDITORS AND TRANSLATORS

WANDA BOEKE (1954) grew up in Massachusetts, where she was born to Dutch parents. After obtaining an Master of Fine Arts in translation from the University of Iowa, she went as a Fulbright scholar to The Netherlands, to study and work with James S. Holmes. She works as a freelance translator, editor, and an instructor of English as a Second Language/DSL instructor.

ERICA EIJSKER (1949), coeditor of this collection, studied Dutch at the University of Amsterdam, where she received a Master of Arts in drama. In 1986 she happened to be in New York when two volumes of the Defiant Muse series were being presented. She could not resist the temptation to do all she could to add Dutch flowers to the bouquet.

SHEILA GOGOL (1942) was born in New York. Her first ambition was to be a poet. While traveling throughout the world, she met and married a Dutch man in Amsterdam, where she has worked as a translator and has been teaching for decades.

MARJOLIJN DE JAGER (1936) was born in Borneo, Indonesia, and raised after the war in Amsterdam. She immigrated with her parents to the United States in 1958. She has published translations from the Dutch, primarily of poems by Hanny Michaelis, in a number of magazines in the United States and Canada, and several of her translations in *Poet Lore* have received special awards for excellence.

RIA LOOHUIZEN (1944) worked as an editor for a Dutch publisher before she moved to San Francisco. There she founded Twin Peaks Press and published work by Dutch poets. After returning to The Netherlands she continued translating Dutch poetry into English.

MAAIKE MEIJER (1949), editor of this anthology, was born in The Netherlands and lives in Amsterdam. She translated Adrienne Rich's poetry into Dutch and wrote an influential Ph.D. dissertation on feminist theories of reading and Dutch women poets after the Second World War: *De lust tot lezen (Lust for letters)* in 1988. She is an associate professor of women's studies at the University of Utrecht and professor at the University of Maastricht in the same field.

ANKIE PEYPERS (1928), coeditor of this anthology, is also a contributor to the collection. See her biography in "Notes on the Poets."

ANNEKE PRINS (1934) is lecturer in Dutch language and literature at Columbia University in New York. Her translation *Medieval Dutch Drama: Four Secular Plays and Four Farces from the Van Hulthem Manuscript* is forthcoming from Pegasus Press in the series "Medieval and Renaissance Drama Texts in Translation."

JOHANNA W. PRINS (1927) holds master's degrees in library science and art history and worked for several decades as curator of the slide collection at Syracuse University. She has published translations of Jacob Cats and Roemer Visscher and has cotranslated various contemporary Dutch women writers. She and her daughter Johanna H. (Yopie) Prins immigrated to the United States from Holland in 1968.

JOHANNA H. (YOPIE) PRINS (1959), coeditor of this anthology, pursued translation studies at the University of Amsterdam as a Fulbright Scholar and received a Ph.D. in comparative literature from Princeton University. She is assistant professor of English and comparative literature at the University of Michigan. Prins has coedited *Dwelling in Possibility: Women Poets and Critics on Poetry* (1997), and is the author of *Victorian Sappho,* forthcoming from Princeton University Press.

MYRA SCHOLZ (1944) studied German and Dutch literature at Indiana University in Bloomington, and Dutch language and literature at the Free University of Amsterdam. She now works as a freelance translator and editor and as a private teacher of English.

RINA VERGANO (1953) was born in Hammersmith, grew up in South London suburbia and worked on various youth projects and at the Round House Theatre before moving to The Netherlands in 1980. She has translated numerous Dutch pieces for the theater and film, including several works by Alex van Warmerdam. She lives in Amsterdam with her husband and three children.

The following translators contributed single translations: Adriaan Barnouw, the medieval ballad of Sir Halewin; Mother Columba Hart, a poem by the beguine and mystic Hadewijch; Tony Briggs, a poem by Anna Roemers Visscher and one by Elizabeth Wolff-Bekker; André Lefevere, two poems by Henriette Roland Holst; Scott Rollins, a poem by Christine D'haen; Marcus Cumberlege, idem.; Carla van Splunteren, a poem by Ellen Warmond; Maria Jacobs, idem.; Manfred Wolf, two poems by Ellen Warmond and one by Fritzi ten Harmsen van Beek; John Rudge, a poem by Judith Herzberg; Shirley Kaufman, idem.; and Greta Kilburn, a poem by Fritzi ten Harmsen van Beek.

Elisabeth Eybers and Ankie Peypers translated some of their own poems. Sonja Pos translated her own poems, in collaboration with Ankie Peypers and Wanda Boeke.

CREDITS

For permission to reprint and translate the poems in this anthology, we acknowledge with thanks the following publishers, poets, and translators:

Anonymous, "Sir Halewin he sang a song," translated as "An Old Ballad of Sir Halewin," by Adriaan Barnouw, from *Coming After: An Anthology of Poetry from the Low Countries,* ed. A. J. Barnouw (New Brunswick: Rutgers University Press, 1948). Reprinted by permission of Rutgers University Press.

Hadewijch, "The Paradoxes of Love," translated by Mother Columba Hart, from Hadewijch, *The Complete Works,* translated and with an introduction by Mother Columba Hart O. S. B. (London: SPCK). ©1980 by the Missionary Society of St. Paul the Apostle in the State of New York. Reprinted by permission of Paulist Press.

Henriette Roland Holst-Van der Schalk, "Ik wil niet meer als vroeger tot U gaan" from *Jeugdwerk 1884–1892* (Amsterdam: Meulenhoff, 1969); "Over het ontwaken mijner ziel" from *Sonnetten en verzen in terzinen geschreven* (Rotterdam: Brusse, 1913); "Moeder van visschers" from *De nieuwe geboort,* (Amsterdam: Brusse, 1928). Reprinted by permission of Stichting Henriette Roland Holst te Heerenveen, M. Stuiveling-van Vierssen Trip.

Julia Tulkens, "Wissenbos" from *Het huis van de stilte* (Drongen bij Gent: Colibrant, 1959). Reprinted by permission of the poet.

Anna Blaman, "A la Omar Khayyam" and "Dans" from *Mijn eigen zelf* (Amsterdam: Meulenhoff, 1977). Reprinted by permission of de Erven Anna Blaman, Johanna Petronella Vrugt.

Ida Gerhardt, "Biografisch," "De ratten," "Voor M. Vasalis," "Archaïsche grafsteen," and "Sappho" from *Verzamelde gedichten* (Amsterdam: Athenaeum-Polak and Van Gennep, 1985). Reprinted by permission of the poet.

Clara Eggink, "De heks" from *Schiereiland* (Den Haag: L. J. C. Boucher, 1938). Reprinted by permission of the poet.

Annie M. G. Schmidt, "Erwtjes," "Moeder dicht," "Biologie," and "Zeur niet" from *Tot hier toe: Gedichten en liedjes voor toneel, radio en televisie 1938–1985* (Amsterdam: Querido, 1987). Reprinted by permission of the poet and the publisher.

Elisabeth Eybers, "Brontë, Dickinson & Kie" from *Onderdak* (Amsterdam: Querido, 1969); "Inspirasie" and "So-Called" from *Respyt* (Amsterdam: Querido, 1993); "Kreet" from *Tydverdryf/Pastime* (Amsterdam: Querido, 1996). Reprinted by permission of the poet.

Hella S. Haasse, "Virgo" from *Stroomversnelling* (Amsterdam: Querido, 1945); "Ik zag Cassandra in 't Concertgebouw" from Nel Noordzij, *Nederlandse dichteressen na 1900* (Amsterdam: De Bezige Bij, 1957). Reprinted by permission of the poet.

Hanny Michaelis, "Eierschalen tot de rand gevuld" from *Water uit de rots* (Amsterdam: Van Oorschot, 1973); "De triomfantelijke moeders" and "Drie jaar was ik ongeveer" from *De rots van Gibraltar* (Amsterdam: Van Oorschot, 1969); "Ergens in huis" and "Je gezicht onherkenbaar" from *Wegdraven naar een nieuw utopia* (Amsterdam: Van Oorschot, 1971). Reprinted by permission of the poet.

Christine D'haen, "Argo" from *Mirages* (Amsterdam: Querido, 1989). Reprinted by permission of the poet. Translation by Marcus Cumberlege from *Dietsche Warande en Belfort* (March/April, 1983), 111. Reprinted with minor changes by permission of the translator. "Derde grafgedicht voor Kira van Kasteel" and "Negende grafgedicht voor Kira van Kasteel" from *Onyx* (Amsterdam: Athenaeum-Polak and Van Gennep, 1983). Reprinted by permission of the poet. "The ninth epitaph for Kira van Kasteel," translated by Scott Rollins, from *Poetry in Flanders Now*, selected by E. van Viet and W. Roggeman (Flemish PEN-Centre, 1982). Reprinted with changes by permission of the translator.

Nel Noordzij, "Gebed van een hoer" from *Leven zonder opperhuid* (Amsterdam: De Bezige Bij, 1962). Reprinted by permission of the poet.

Fritzi ten Harmsen van der Beek, "Op mijn dertigste verjaardag" and "Interpretatie van het uitzicht" from *Geachte muizenpoot en achttien andere gedichten* (Amsterdam: De Bezige Bij, 1977). Reprinted by permission of the publisher. "On My Thirtieth Birthday," translated by Manfred Wolf, from *The Shape of Houses* (Berkeley: Two Window Press, 1974). Reprinted by permission of the translator.

Ankie Peypers, "Hij," "Voorbeschikking," "Muizen," and "Waarschuwing" from *Gedichten 1951–1975* (Amsterdam: An Dekker, 1991); "Brief" from *Brieven, motieven & juffrouw Vonk.* (Baarn: De Prom, 1987). Reprinted by permission of the poet.

Ellen Warmond, "Schipbreuk" from *Tegenspeler tijd* (Amsterdam: Querido, 1979); "Modern times" from *Testbeeld voor een koud klimaat* (Amsterdam:

Querido, 1966); "Humanisme voor kleinbehuisden" and "In antwoord op uw schrijven" from *Geen bloemen/geen bezoek* (Amsterdam: Querido, 1968). Reprinted by permission of the poet. "Modern times," translated by Maria Jacobs, from *With Other Words: A Bilingual Anthology of Contemporary Dutch Poetry by Women* ed. by Maria Jacobs (Windsor, Ontario: Netherlandic Press, 1985). Reprinted with changes by permission of the translator. "Humanism for Those Who Live in Cramped Quarters" and "In Reply to Your Letter," translated by Manfred Wolf, from *The Shape of Houses* (Berkeley: Two Windows Press, 1974). Reprinted with changes by permission of the translator.

Andreas Burnier, "Op zoek naar Gertrude Stein" from *Na de laatste keer* (Amsterdam: Querido, 1981). Reprinted by permission of the poet.

Loes Nobel, "nostalgie" from *Tussen sneeuw en lava* (Amsterdam: De Beuk, 1975); "het zijn de zwarte schimmen" from *En kraters sloten de ogen* (Amsterdam: De Beuk, 1977); "en na de indaling" from *Morgen word je geboren* (Amsterdam: De Beuk, 1983). Reprinted by permission of the poet.

Judith Herzberg, "Bad Zwischenahn, 1964" and "Afwasmachine" from *Beemdgras* (Amsterdam: Van Oorschot, 1980); "Minnaars minnaars" from *Dagrest* (Amsterdam: Van Oorschot, 1987); "De zeeman" from *Botshol* (Amsterdam: Van Oorschot, 1981). Reprinted by permission of the poet. "Bad Zwischenahn, 1964" translated by Shirley Kaufman with Judith Herzberg, published in *But What: Selected Poems* (Oberlin, Ohio: Oberlin College Press, 1988). Reprinted by permission of the publisher. "The dishwasher" translated by John Rudge, published in *Dutch Interior* (New York: Columbia University Press, 1984). Reprinted by permission of the translator.

Sonja Pos, "Tijd" and "De laatste trede" from *De eigen tijd* (Amsterdam: Contact, 1988). Reprinted by permission of the poet.

Elly de Waard, "De ribben van de brug liggen," "Op zilveren voeten trippelt," "Wie kan Plato's Symposion nog," "Anadyomene" and "De bergen roken van de herfst" from *Een Wildernis van verbindingen* (Amsterdam: De Harmonie, 1986). Reprinted by permission of the poet.

Erika Dedinszky, "Pinkstermorgen" from *Kornoeljeboom* (Haarlem: Uitgevers maatschappij Holland, 1975). Reprinted by permission of the poet.

Neeltje Maria Min, from the cycle "Een vrouw bezoeken"—IV: "Kapok. Het opklapbed. Verloren tijd?," V: "Diep in de put waar haar gebeente ligt," VII: "Een jurk met stroken van satijn," VIII "Haar schaduw was mijn onderdak," and IX: "De kamer is er een op schaal" from *Een vrouw bezoeken* (Amsterdam: Bert Bakker, 1985). Reprinted by permission of the poet.

Christa Eelman, "Toen ik opkeek" from *Over niet meer kunnen* (Amsterdam: Sara, 1981).

Anna Enquist, "Conversatie met de kinderen" and "Vanuit de keuken" from *Soldatenliederen* (Amsterdam: Arbeiderspers, 1991). Reprinted by permission of the poet.

Astrid Roemer, "wend niet het gezicht af—mijn moeder" and "zij zien ons vergaan als mislukte oogst" from *NoordzeeBlues* (Breda: De Geus, 1985). Reprinted by permission of the poet.

Carla Bogaards, "De reigers van Amsterdam, de hertogin en de zebra's" from *De reigers van Amsterdam* (Amsterdam: An Dekker, 1987). Reprinted by permission of the poet.

Maja Panajotova, "Taal" from *Verzwegen alibi* (Antwerpen: Manteau, 1983). Reprinted by permission of the poet.

Miriam Van hee, "straks komt het sneeuwen" and "ze wou dat ze iets terugvond" from *Ingesneeuwd* (Amsterdam: De Bezige Bij, 1984). Reprinted by permission of the poet.

Ineke Van Mourik, "In de paskamer van V & D," and Eva Van Sonderen, "Prinsjesdag," from Elly de Waard, ed., *De nieuwe wilden in de poëzie* (Amsterdam: Sara/De Harmonie, 1987). Reprinted by permission of the poets.

Chawwa Wijnberg, "als mannen zouden bloeden" and "mijn lief, ik vaar een schip vol tranen" from *Aan mij is niets te zien* (Amsterdam: Furie, 1989). Reprinted by permission of the poet.

Annemarie de Waard, "Stel dat wij van Atlantis kwamen" from *Als Troje: Gedichten* (Baarn: De Prom, 1989). Reprinted by permission of the poet.

Sjuul Deckwitz, "Aan de kade staat een huis," "De gems," "Babette," "Zij huilt. Zij lacht.," and "Wij zijn nachtdynamo's" from *Niet wachten op ontspanning* (Amsterdam: De Bonte Was, 1985). Reprinted by permission of the poet.

Unless otherwise noted above, all translations were made for this anthology and are used by permission of the translators. Every effort has been made to reach all copyright holders for permissions. Any copyright holders not mentioned here are invited to contact the editors through The Feminist Press.

Copyright in the translations not listed above is in the names of the translators.

Additional Sources in the Public Domain:

Anonymous, "Heer Halewyn zong een liedekyn" from Jop Pollmann, ed., *Van tweeërlei minne: Bloemlezing van Middelnederlandse lyriek* (Zwolle: Tjeenk Willink, 1962).

Anonymous, "Het daghet inden Oosten" and "Den dach en wil niet verborghen zijn," from K. Vellekoop en H. Wagenaar-Nolthenius, ed., *Het Antwerps liedboe,* (Amsterdam: Vereniging voor Nederlandse Muziekgeschiedenis, 1975).

Anonymous, "Die nachtegael die sanck een liedt" from Fl. van Duyse, *Het oude Nederlandsche lied: Wereldlijke en geestelijke liederen uit vroegeren tijd* (Den Haag/Antwerpen: Nijhoff, 1905).

Anonymous, "De ploegtrekker" from Harrie Franken, *500 liederen en dansen uit de Kempen* (Zuid-Nederlandse Historische Uitgeverij, 1980).

Anonymous, "Anne Marieken" from J. F. Willems, *Oude Vlaemsche Liederen.* (Gent: Gyselynck, 1848).

Hadewijch, "Lied V" from Hadewijch, *Strofische gedichten: Middelnederlandse tekst en omzetting in modern Nederlands met een inleiding door prof. dr. N. de Paepe* (Leiden: Martinus Nijhoff, 1983); "Negende brief" from Hadewijch, *Brieven,* ed. F. van Bladel, S. J. and B. Spaapen, S. J. (Den Haag: Lannoo, 1954); "De paradoxen van de liefde" from Hadewijch, *Mengeldichten* ed. Dr. J. van Mierlo (Leuven, no year).

Anna Bijns, Refereyn XXVII, "Het waer goet houwen, maer tsorgen es de plage" from Anna Bijns, *Nieuwe Refereinen,* ed. W. J. A. Jonckbloet en W. L. Van Helten, first piece (Groningen: Wolters, 1880).

Anna Roemers Visscher, "Aen Juffrouwe Anna Maria Schuermans" from Fr. Kossman, ed., *Gedichten van Anna Roemers Visscher.* (Den Haag: Martinus Nijhoff, 1925); "Aen Juffrouw Johanna Comans," "Aen Juffvrouw Georgette de Monteneij," and "Muyterij tegen Cupido" from N. Beets, ed., *Alle de gedichten van Anna Roemers Visscher, vol. 2* (Utrecht: J. L. Beijers, 1881).

Maria Tesselschade Roemers Visscher, "Uytdaging (aen M. D.)" from J. A. Worp, ed., *Een onwaardeerlijcke vrouw: Brieven en verzen van en aan Maria Tesselschade.* ('s Gravenhage: Martinus Nijhoff, 1918).

Katharina Questiers, "Aan J. D. H. Doen hij sijn Robijn voor mijn Diamant-Ringh wilde ruylen" and "Aen Jufre Cornelia van der Veer" from *Lauwerstryt tusschen Catharina Questiers en Cornelia van der Veer* (Amsterdam: Adriaen Veenendael, 1665).

Elisabeth Koolaert-Hoofman, "Bruin boven blond" from *Keur van Nederlandsche letteren,* second part, fourth piece (Amsterdam, no year).

Zara Maria van Zon, "Bestendigheid van 't onbestendige" from *Verzameling van stichtelyke gedichten, nagelaten door wylen de welgeborene jonkvrouwe Zara Maria van Zon* (Utrecht: J. H. Vonk van Lynden, 1756).

Juliana Cornelia de Lannoy, "De onbestendigheid," "Lijcaön," and "Aan de Heeren Bestuurderen der Maatschappij van Dichtkunde te 's Gravenhage" from *Dichtkundige werken* (Leyden: Abraham and Jan Honkoop, 1780); "De volmaakte man," from *Nagelaten dichtwerken* (Leyden: Abraham and Jan Honkoop, 1783).

Elizabeth Wolff-Bekker, "Aan Mejuffrouw Agatha Deken" from *Mengelpoëzy,* vol. 3 (Amsterdam, 1786).

Agatha Deken, "Vriendschapszucht" from Maria Bosch and Agatha Deken, *Stichtelijke gedichten van Maria Bosch en Agatha Deken* (Amsterdam, 1775).

Katharina Wilhelmina Bilderdijk-Schweickhardt, "Grafschrift op Robespierre" and "Op het afsterven van ons derde dochtertjen, Adelheide Irene, naar haar twee overleden zusjens, genoemd" from *De dichtwerken van Vrouwe Katharina Wilhelmina Bilderdijk,* vol. 3 (Haarlem: A. C. Krusemann, 1858, 1859, 1860).

Giza Ritschl, "Eens danste ik in een Csárda" from *Keur uit liefdeverzen.* (Maastricht: A. A. M. Stols, 1939).